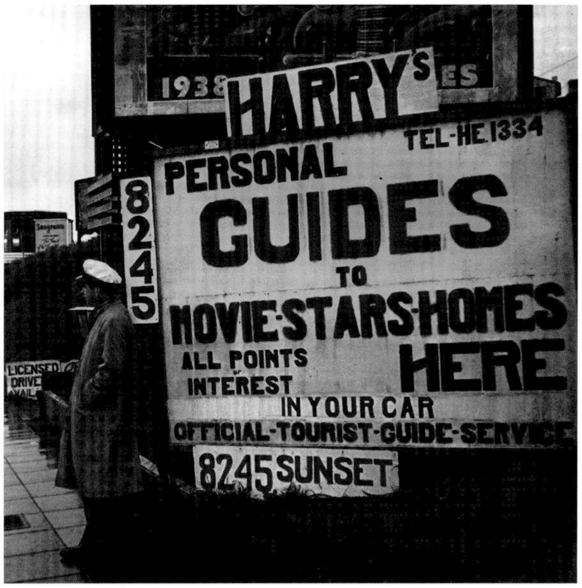
HARRY'S
TEL-HE.1334
PERSONAL
GUIDES
TO
MOVIE-STARS-HOMES
ALL POINTS
INTEREST
HERE
IN YOUR CAR
OFFICIAL-TOURIST-GUIDE-SERVICE
8245 SUNSET
8245
1938
LICENSED
DRIVE

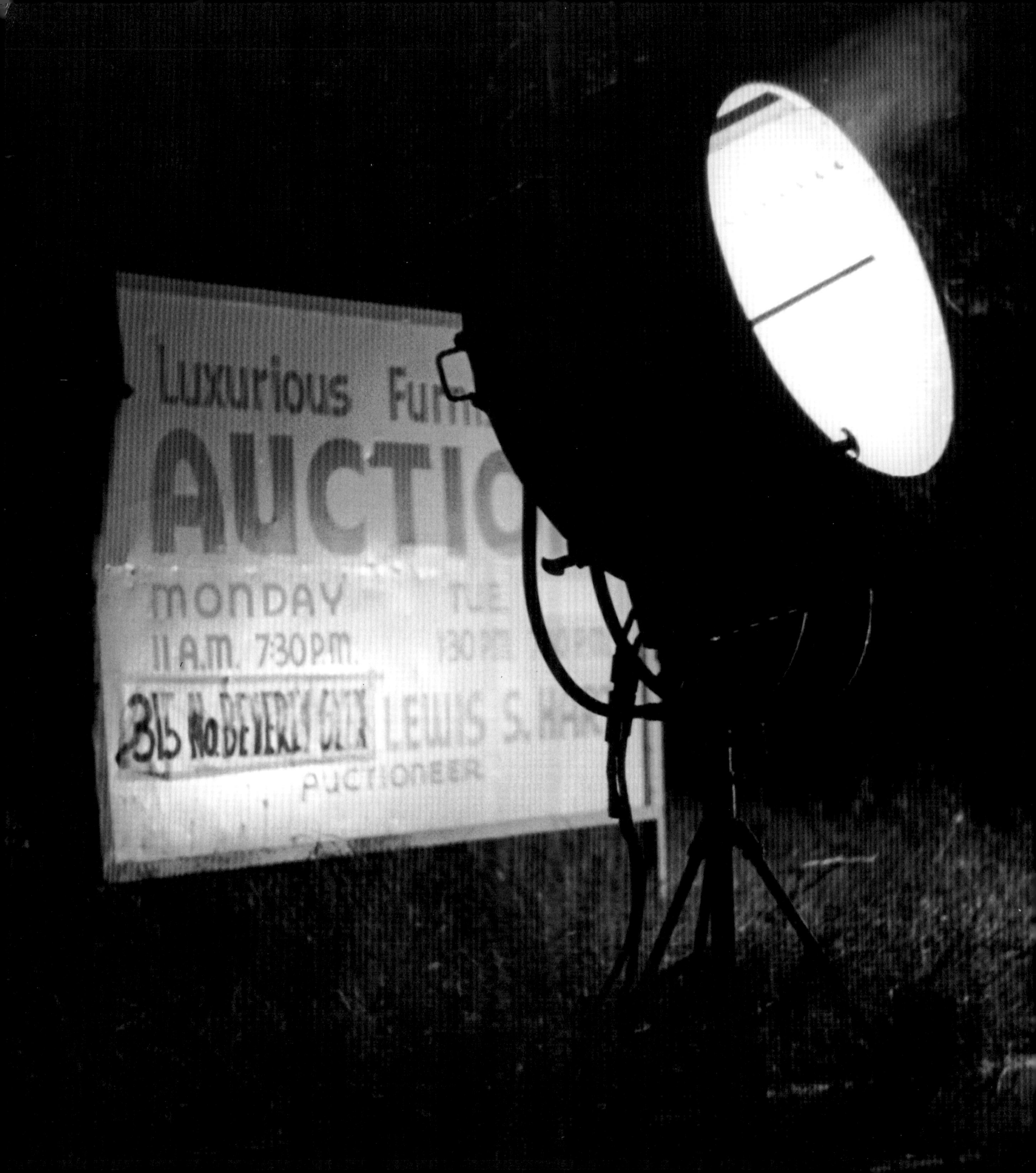
Luxurious
MONDAY
11 A.M. 7:30 P.M.
AUCTIONEER

Camera Over Hollywood

Photographs by John Swope 1936–1938

Introduction by Dennis Hopper

Essay by Graham Howe

Distributed Art Publishers

All rights reserved. No part of this book may be reproduced or
transmitted in any form or by any means, electronic or mechanical,
including photocopying or recording, or by any information retrieval system,
without written permission from the copyright holders, except for
brief passages quoted by a reviewer in a newspaper or magazine.

©1999 D.A.P./Distributed Art Publishers, Inc.
155 Sixth Avenue, New York, NY 10013
Tel 212-627-1999 Fax 212-627-9484
All Rights Reserved

Printed in China
First Printing 1999
ISBN 1-891024-08-6

BOOK PRODUCTION:
Curatorial Assistance, Inc., Los Angeles

EDITORIAL DIRECTOR: Graham Howe
ESSAY EDITOR: Rod Slemmons
COPY EDITOR: David Greene
GRAPHIC DESIGN: Karen Bowers
PHOTOGRAPH DIGITIZATION: Robert Kranzke and Alex Mendoza
EDITORIAL PRODUCTION: Craig Johnson

For information on the traveling exhibition of *Camera Over Hollywood,* please contact
Curatorial Assistance, Inc., 113 East Union Street, Pasadena, CA 91103
Tel 626-577-9696 Fax 626-449-9603 E-mail curatorial@curatorial.com

All photographs in this publication ©1999 The John Swope Trust
An American in Hollywood ©1999 by Graham Howe
Introduction © 1999 by Dennis Hopper

Front cover:
Albertina Rasch Dancers at MGM, 1938

Half title:
Guides to the Stars, Sunset Boulevard (detail),1938

Frontispiece:
Real estate auction sign and Klieg light, 1938

Opposite:
Main Street, Los Angeles, 1938

Back Cover:
Jimmy Stewart signing autographs for fans, 1938

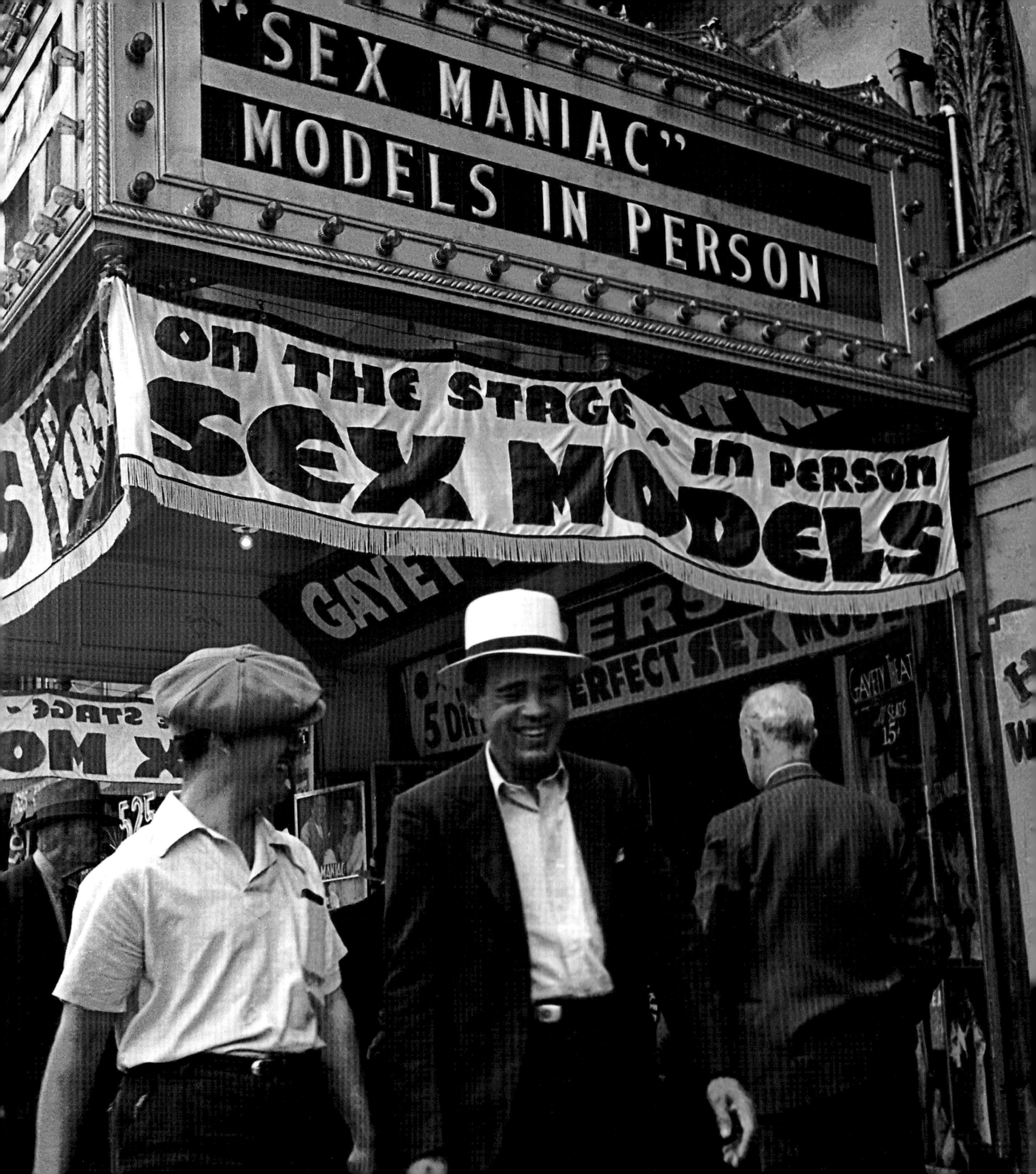
"SEX MANIAC"
MODELS IN PERSON
ON THE STAGE
SEX MODELS
IN PERSON
GAYETY

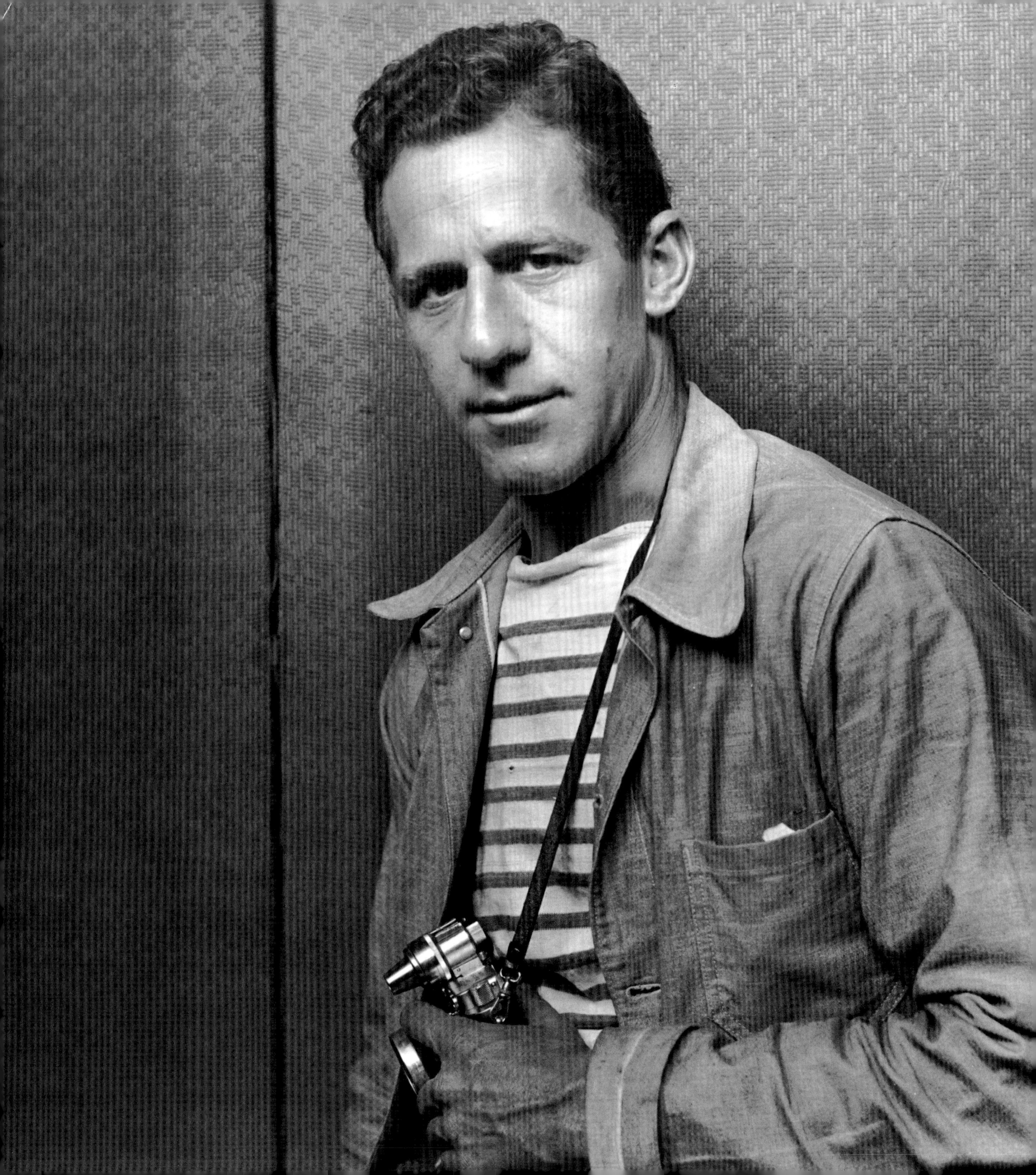

Acknowledgments

In 1979 my father, John Swope, died, leaving an enormous collection of photographs. The Swope family's wish has been to organize his work so that museums and educational institutions could exhibit his extraordinary achievement. In 1993 we engaged Graham Howe, director of Curatorial Assistance, to help us organize and direct the collection. Because of the vastness of this body of work, I soon realized that it would be a full-time job and made the decision to dedicate my energies towards managing the archives. It has been a remarkable adventure, and in the process I have realized a great many things about my father's life and work that I hadn't known before.

This book and the accompanying traveling exhibition could not have been accomplished without the support and collaboration of many exceptional and talented individuals. I would like to extend my appreciation to the following people who were instrumental in realizing this project.

First, I owe a special debt to the late Roddy McDowall. Sadly, his death late last year prevented him from contributing his promised writing about the life and photographic work of my father. I wish to thank Keenan Behrle for his lifetime of guidance and support for the Swope family, and to Elsa Rady, whose judgment and advice has enhanced this project in immeasurable ways. My thanks go to Gerald and the late Virginia Oppenheimer for their generous support of the traveling exhibition and computer viewing station enabling visitors to see the collection in depth through digital technology. Craig Krull of the Craig Krull Gallery, Santa Monica, is ever appreciated for his unfailing support of my late father's work. Norman Lloyd kindly granted interviews enabling us to gather his personal recollections of John that were invaluable to this project. He also reminded me of my father's contagious laugh. Thanks go to Rod Slemmons, whose editing expertise gave full form to Graham Howe's essay and to Miles Kreuger for his fact checking of the Hollywood era. Thanks also go to Dennis Hopper for sharing his remembrances of John.

And to my mother, Dorothy McGuire, John's biggest fan, who has tirelessly promoted his work for all the right reasons, thank you. And to my sister, Topo, who like me also recognizes threads of her life interwoven in John's work.

We have just started. There will be more books and other projects from this multifaceted and unusually rich collection that continues to render treasures vital to the legacy of my father and to the medium of photography.

Mark Swope
Los Angeles, February 28, 1999

John Swope (self-portrait), 1937

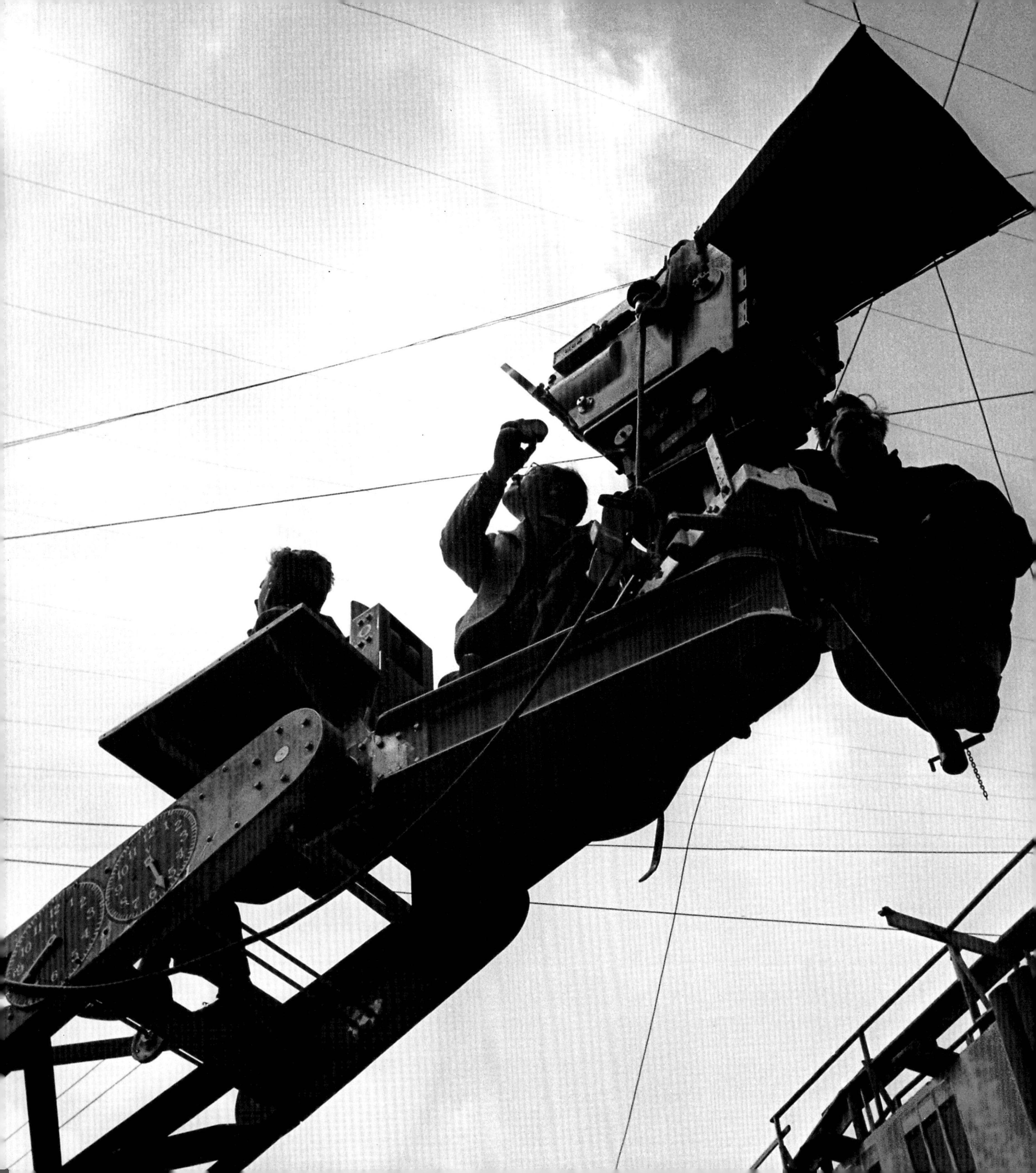

Introduction

by DENNIS HOPPER

John Swope was elegant, quiet, intelligent, steadfast. I still see his pipe-smoking silhouette outlined poolside at the Valencia Hotel in La Jolla just above the Cove with his wife, Dorothy McGuire, or sitting in the darkened theater when he was my boss and executive producer of the La Jolla Playhouse. It was 1952. I was 16. John was already a *LIFE* photographer, having taken the famous shot of Brando (cover of *LIFE* magazine) in a toga from *Julius Caesar,* the film.

Dorothy starred in the production of *I am a Camera,* a play by Christopher Isherwood at the playhouse. I was on curtain and so enthralled with her performance that I would miss my cue to bring the curtain down, leaving the actors standing helplessly on stage. John confronted me and told me I was not to pull curtain ever again, but that I was to continue picking up props in the pickup truck. We were out back of the theater. I told John how sorry I was that I missed the cue and that I would be on my toes from now on, whereupon I opened the door of the pickup, got in the driver's seat, started it, and put it in reverse. John stood in front of the pickup where I had left him, watching as I started to back up fast. I noticed the look on his smiling face turn to horror as I backed up, smashing the pickup into a telephone pole. Poor John threw his arms in the air in disbelief and just went off muttering to himself. I didn't lose my job, but I was so starstruck that I was definitely a liability.

The next year John and Dorothy came to see me perform as Lorenzo in *The Merchant of Venice* at the Old Globe Theater in San Diego. I then went to John and asked him if he could introduce me to a casting director or someone in the movie business. I knew only the people I had met at the playhouse, who were mostly actors. So John formed a letter of introduction to Ruth Birch, head of casting at Hal Roach Studios. I was 18. She gave me a ten-line part in a *Cavalcade of America,* which got me my SAG card and an agent.

John Swope is responsible for getting me started as a professional actor. I will always be in his debt for that and for giving me the opportunity to work with Hank Milam and Vincent Price at the playhouse in La Jolla. These three are the ones who gave me my first real education in art and photography. I am more than indebted to these gentlemen. My foundation in the arts I owe to them. That letter from John took me from the depths of creative poverty to a rich life in culture and the arts. John was a great photographer of the golden age of Hollywood and much more. Use your eyes—it's obvious.

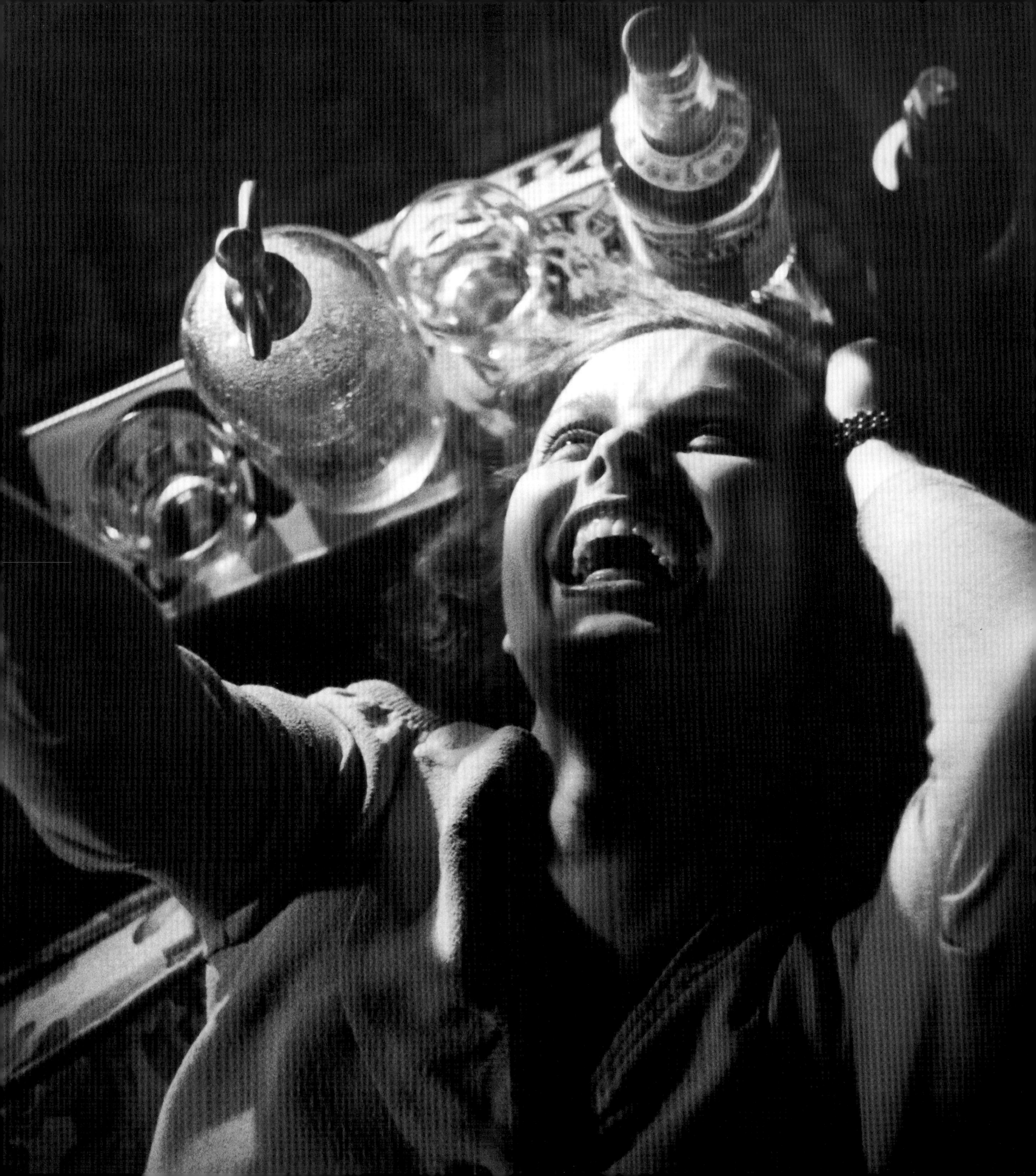

An American in Hollywood

Graham Howe

Like his contemporary Walker Evans, John Swope came to photography via a circuitous route from a position of privilege. Uninspired by the expectations of his financially successful family, he used his socially elevated position as a platform from which to observe—and occasionally satirize—his times and social milieu. He found the camera, which allows for simultaneous intense inclusion and quiet observation, an ideal instrument. Unlike Evans, who preferred to find evidence of America's self-invention at the edges, Swope went straight to Hollywood, the bright generator of illusion and mythology.

Producer Leland Hayward initially hired Swope as an assistant producer and occasional publicity photographer for his stable of actors, directors, and writers in 1930s Hollywood. But Swope was more interested in a layered exploration of Hollywood as a culture—especially behind the scenes—and did far more than was expected or even desired of him by Hayward. According to Hayward, "John Swope's single idea, from the moment he began, was to show Hollywood 'as it is,' though he never used those words."[1] Good luck and Hayward's provisional indulgence allowed him to produce the body of work that resulted in *Camera Over Hollywood,* first published in 1939.

There was a limit to Hayward's benefaction in spite of his being intrigued by Swope's attitudes and images. He was, after all, supposed to be running a film production business. After about eighteen months Hayward drew the line. He called Swope into his office and renegotiated his contract to allocate him a half-time position, hoping that Swope would do his personal work on his own time. In actuality, this resulted in an even less equitable balance to Hayward, since the personal work depended on Swope being in the same place at the same time as the paid work. "I [got only] one hour a day of John's time. I tried to work this out twenty-four different ways but was finally unable to find an hour that seemed to work out even moderately well for him—so we parted."[2]

But by the time this happened, in 1938, Swope had accumulated a sufficiently cohesive portfolio of photographs to show Bennett Cerf, president of Random House, New York, who offered to publish his first book. Over the next few months, Swope dedicated himself to completing his vision for the publication. He added a few more photographs,

---

Laughing girl, Hollywood party, 1938

wrote captions for the pictures, and compiled some technical data on the making of his photographs. He then bravely asked Hayward to write the introduction. Even though he had unwillingly paid for the work that resulted in *Camera Over Hollywood,* Leland Hayward formally acknowledged Swope's creative achievement.

The popularity of filmed entertainment in the 1930s was immense and universal. The film industry, seemingly immune from the economic ravages of the Great Depression, was controlled by the "Big Eight" Hollywood studios: Metro-Goldwyn-Mayer, Warner Brothers, 20th Century-Fox, Columbia, Paramount, RKO, Universal, and United Artists. Newspapers and magazines, fed a constant diet of photographs and text, cashed in on the public's fascination with the glamour and sex of the stars. Hollywood's powerful attraction as the epicenter of the movies drew an endless stream of aspiring actors and would-be movie talent looking for access to fame and fortune. Photographs, in the form of studio stills, provided the fans a surrogate brush with their long list of idols: Greta Garbo, Spencer Tracy, Clark Gable, Marlene Dietrich, Norma Shearer, Jean Harlow, Joan Crawford, William Powell, Myrna Loy, Jeanette MacDonald, Robert Taylor, Nelson Eddy, Errol Flynn, John Barrymore, Cary Grant, Lucille Ball, Fred Astaire, Ginger Rogers, Bing Crosby, Mae West, the Marx Brothers, Shirley Temple, and Jane Withers.

This was Hollywood's late golden era. Important films released from 1936 to 1938 included *Lost Horizon, The Awful Truth,* and *You Can't Take It With You* (Columbia), *A Star Is Born* (David O. Selznick—United Artists release), *Stage Door* and *Winterset* (RKO), *Dead End* and *The Hurricane* (Samuel Goldwyn—United Artists release) *Boys Town, Romeo and Juliet, Captains Courageous* and *Marie Antoinette,* (MGM), *The Life of Emile Zola* (Warner Brothers), and *Alexander's Ragtime Band* and *In Old Chicago* (20th Century-Fox). Also rising at this time, the Disney Studio released *Snow White and the Seven Dwarfs* in 1937.

In 1936, the year of Swope's arrival in Hollywood, Blaise Cendrars (1887–1961), one of France's most gifted writers, also came to Hollywood with the idea of critically observing and documenting this "Mecca of the Movies." Cendrars' stay was all of two weeks while Swope's work carried over two years, and they each saw Hollywood from an entirely different angle. Yet remarkably their conclusions about its life and culture are very similar. The "real" face of Hollywood was enigmatic, with its floating population of those wanting and waiting to see and be seen.

With a luxurious apartment at the Roosevelt Hotel as his base, Cendrars set out to visit each of the major studios so that he might write his impressions for the French newspaper *Paris-Soir.* He kept finding himself snubbed by the studio guards, stars, moguls, and other key figures despite his official press capacity and credentials as a writer. He responded by inventing a humorous and satirical part diary, part fairy tale to show how inaccessible Hollywood was to any but the initiated. Understandably, his writings are critical of the studio system as a stereotype of American corporate business.

"In Hollywood, all roads lead . . . to a studio! Here he encounters not a gate but a wall. This wall is the famous Great Wall of China that surrounds every studio and that makes Hollywood, already a difficult city to conquer, a true forbidden city."[3] Entrances to the studios "are nearly impassable for the non initiate, as if, really, to wish to make your way into a studio is to want to force entry into the Holy of Holies."[4] To illustrate his point he quotes a sign above the entrance to Universal Films: "It's useless to wait—It's useless to insist—You're wasting

John Swope (self-portrait), 1937

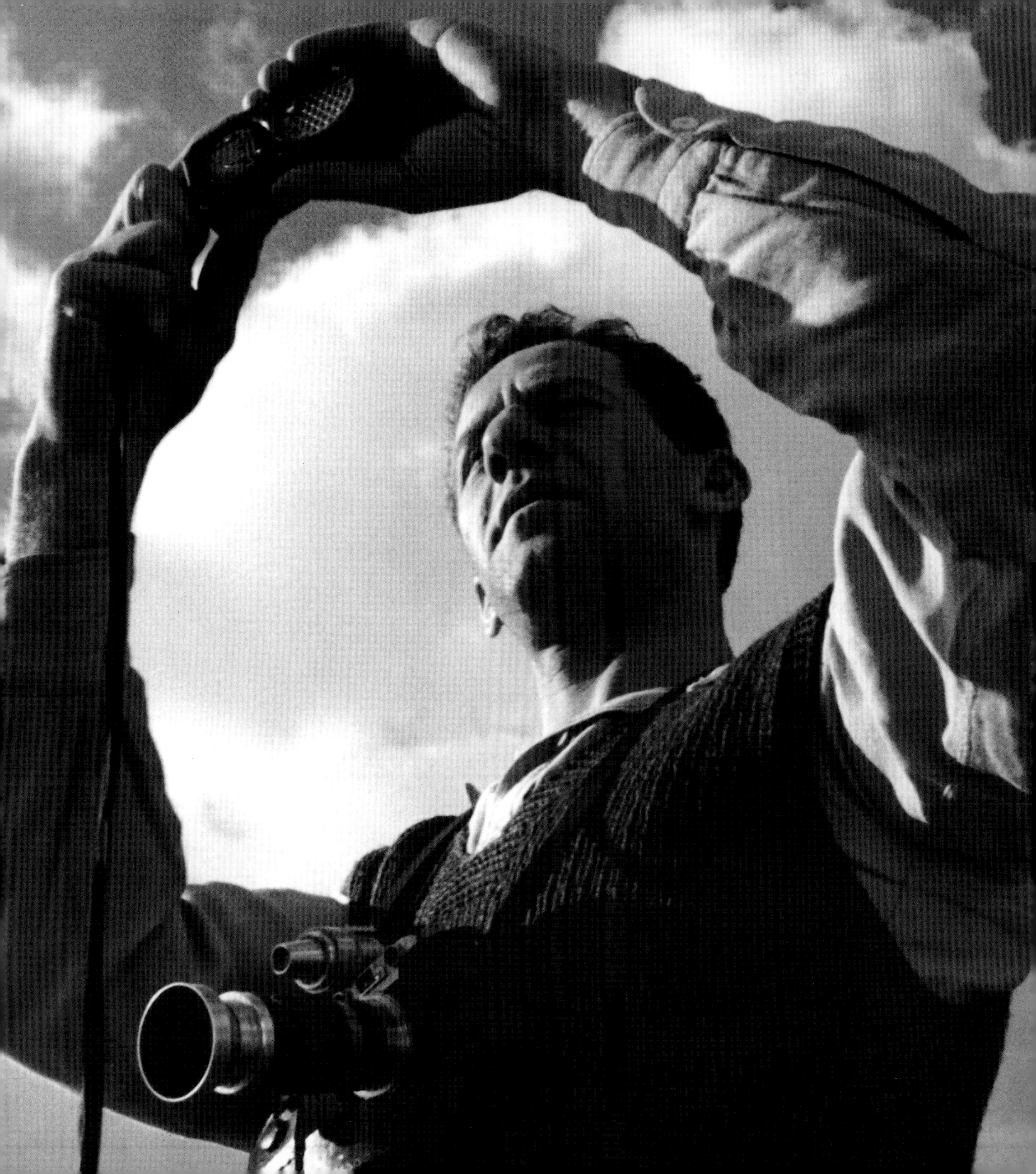

your time—Recommendations won't get you anywhere—This place was not meant for you—Do Not Enter."[5] Access was, to a very large extent, determined by social position, preferably accompanied by talent and charisma—not the other way around.

• • •

Swope was born in 1908 in New Brunswick, New Jersey, the son of Gerard Swope, president of the General Electric Company, the largest corporation in the United States. His New York upbringing was privileged and comfortable. His uncle, Herbert Bayard Swope—one of the first Pulitzer Prize winners for journalism—was the editor of *The World*, one of New York's leading newspapers.

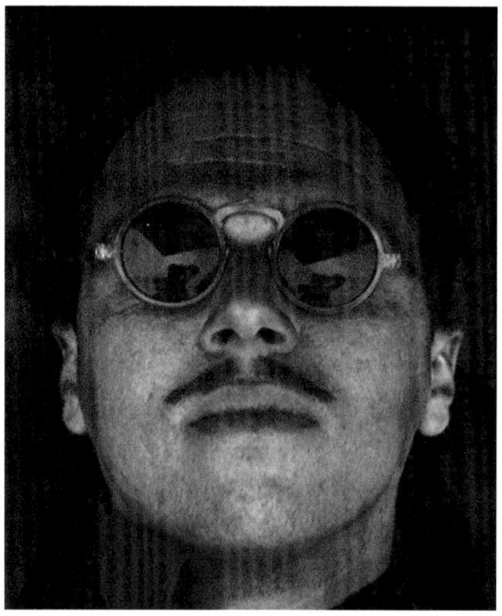

Josh Logan, 1937

During his studies at Harvard University (1926–1930), Swope joined with his friends to create a theatrical group called the University Players Guild. This was a group of Princeton, Harvard, Radcliffe, Vassar, and Smith undergraduates who organized their own summer theater on Cape Cod. Here he met several extraordinarily promising young actors, writers, producers, and directors who became his close friends and whose talents propelled most of them to celebrated careers. Key and closest among his friends at the University Players were Henry Fonda and James Stewart.[6]

As Henry Fonda recalled, "I first set eyes on John Swope in 1928 when I was in the audience [at the Elizabeth Theatre, Cape Cod] and he was on stage playing Mr. Twiller in the hysterically funny George Kelly play, *The Torchbearers.* My laughter was so contagious [to a previously apathetic audience] that I was invited to join them which I did promptly."[7]

The University Players was not the "legitimate theater" that Swope had tried to make it in *The Decennial Report,* a publication that tracked the careers of graduates, but more an endeavor at pure fun. As Jane Alexander reports, "It was really only a step above a college lark. How could it not have been, when they were mostly together for summers, like some kind of extended, organized vacation?"[8] "In one rehearsal of a fight scene, for example, Fonda and Swope were so maladroit about faking punches that the two of them ended up going at each other for real."[9]

Trysts were common among the group, and there was much competition between Jimmy Stewart and Henry Fonda, both of whom had designs on the hot-tempered Margaret Sullavan. The intrigue continued even after Sullavan and Fonda were wed late in 1931, a marriage that was to last only a few months. Heartbroken, Stewart left for Broadway early in 1932 as all the University Players drifted away to various jobs on Broadway or in Hollywood. But by the summer of 1935 Sullavan was married to Leland Hayward. She demanded Jimmy Stewart as her Hollywood costar in the 20th Century-Fox production *The Farmer Takes a Wife.* The network of connections that would gain Swope his entrée to Hollywood had begun.

In the fall of 1933 Swope was offered a position in Washington to take up an appointment in a short-lived government program under President Franklin D. Roosevelt known as the National Recovery Administration. At age twenty-three, his position was as director of National Code Compliance. This involved a highly bureaucratic system of establishing industrial codes for manufacturing and building compliance. His friend Robert Strauss reported that "John was a good organizer and behind his organizing ability lay his tremendous drive."[10]

Just before the demise of the National Recovery Administration in 1935, Swope was recruited by the Resettlement Administration, where he was assigned to evaluate the effectiveness of federal housing programs throughout the country. Here Swope took up photography as part of a documentation process. One of his more interesting assignments led him to Arthurdale, West Virginia, to assess a coal miners' rehousing project favored by Mrs. Roosevelt. According to Strauss, Swope and Mrs. Roosevelt made a point of socializing with the miners and their families, joining in their traditional songs and square dancing with great gusto.

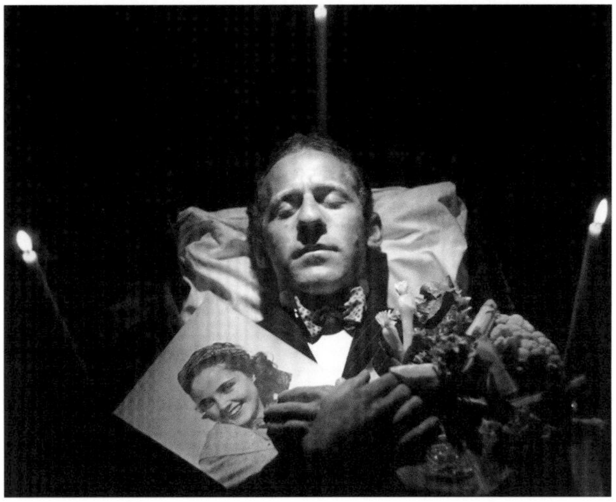

John Swope (self-portrait) playing dead in coffin with photograph of Kay Aldridge, 1937

This ability would help him later. As an American blueblood, John Swope had guaranteed access to the social elite. But he was equally comfortable mingling with the less privileged without condescension. Relying on fundamental warmth, humor, and humanism, the qualities most frequently cited by those who knew him, Swope seemed comfortable anywhere. Even Leland Hayward recognized Swope's special skills, pointing out that he "has had not only to be a great photographer, but a great diplomat."[11] Peter Stackpole, his friend and fellow Hollywood photographer, wrote: "He could photograph the big ones with the freedom of a house guest."[12]

Swope's position with the Resettlement Administration lasted less than a year. In the summer of 1936 he decided to join his friends Henry Fonda and Jimmy Stewart in Hollywood, where they all shared a house in Brentwood. Fonda remembered one of Swope's first photographic efforts in 1936 that confirmed his photographic calling.

"I'm not sure just when John knew he wanted to make photography his life. I do remember about forty-five years ago (1936), when he, Jim Stewart, and I were all single and sharing a house in West Los Angeles, that John was invited to help crew the *Paisano* in the Los Angeles–Honolulu Yacht Race. He took a Leica with him. I know that within a few days after his return he spread out before our popping eyes the most beautiful display of sailing pictures I had ever seen. They were breathtaking. I would like to think that our enthusiasm then had a lot to do with the direction his life was to take."[13]

Swope began his energetic and revealing view of Hollywood when he was twenty-eight years old and had completed his book by the time he was thirty. With his Leica and his own connections and those of his pals Fonda and Stewart, Swope gained carte blanche to photograph Hollywood. His access was legitimized when Hayward hired him.

Swope shows us Hollywood as a working town full of hope, struggle, and success in unequal proportions. He sees the men and women who make the movies as regular folk, be they his friends, the stars, or the would-be actors, extras, and grips waiting for their unemployment checks. But the ironies of Hollywood did not escape Swope. He saw clearly that all these very real people were in the business of creating an elaborate unreality.

Like Robert Frank's view of the disquiet beneath the American postwar prosperity in *The Americans,* Swope shows us a perturbed Hollywood in which nothing seems to fit the fantasy. His formal agility is akin to that of Frank, albeit developed some two decades earlier. He uses his small camera to gain unusual advantage of unsuspecting subjects whose confidence allowed him to disappear. He captures cinematographer giant James Wong Howe (page 49) dwarfed by his camera rig, seemingly more at its mercy than in command. John Barrymore (page 99) in a Shriners parade convertible looks more like a mannequin wheeled past the public than a consummate actor. Swope also shows us moments of genuine tenderness: Jimmy Stewart and Olivia de Havilland (page 95), napping on the grass in the late-day sun, a portable gramophone providing background music to their simple outdoor pleasure. What we see is more like a rehearsal for *It's A Wonderful Life* than real people relaxing: reality as chameleon.

Swope's view of the 1938 Oscar night reveals, in addition to the sanctioned expectation, several other layers of celebrity construction at work (page 133). The official event created for the press to document is the shallow midground of his picture. Louis B. Mayer is passing the Oscar statue to Luise Rainer in the company of Mrs. Spencer Tracy and Frank Capra. Swope is with the press troops in the foreground, joining the silhouettes of his colleagues to his left and right. In the background we see another clutch of press photographers and writers that sandwich and define the event in the middle. Swope's wider view also includes Hollywood's strategy to align with national sentiment embodied in the American flag on the back wall of Hollywood's neoclassical temple.

Swope shows us Hollywood more from the backside than from the façade of the lots and sets. The actual workers seem to spend a lot of their time sleeping. One film extra in period costume actually drinks on the job and sleeps it off between takes. A would-be actress washes her laundry in the sink of her tiny apartment, looking like the lead in a Tennessee Williams plot. John Swope finds the tentacles of fictional comedy and tragedy winding their way into the lives of Hollywood's foot soldiers.

The Swope, Fonda, and Stewart gang (occasionally including Josh Logan) was hell-bent on having as good a life as Hollywood could offer. They attended all the parties, media events, and premieres. Keeping one's self seen was expected by the studios as part of the job. In Swope's case this was an enjoyment in addition to making pictures. Many years later, he recalled the story behind one of his photographs (page 129): "Marion Davies gave a big party for Hearst's seventy-fifth

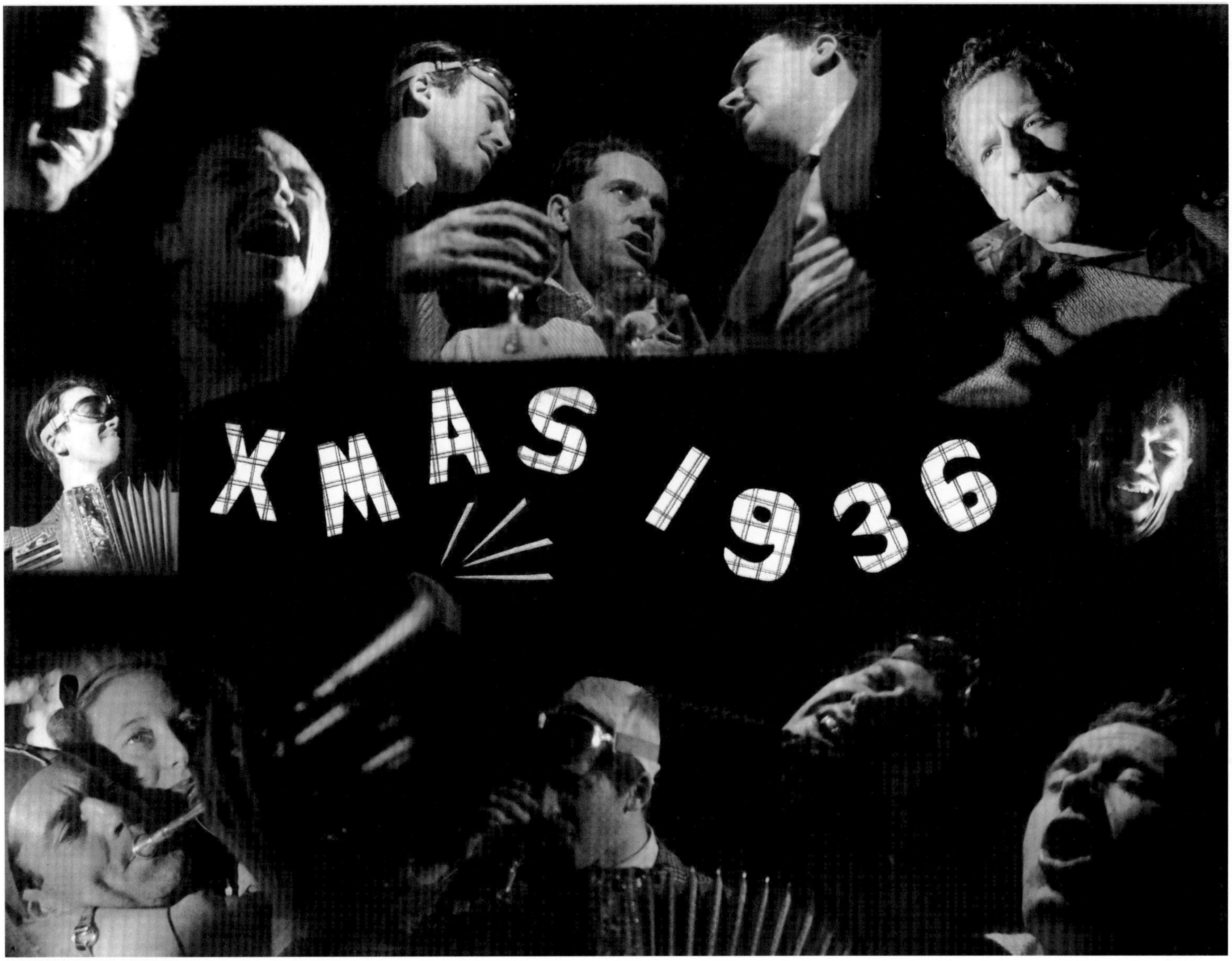

Photo-collage of Henry Fonda, Josh Logan, Jimmy Stewart, and John Swope—group Christmas card, 1936

birthday down at their big home in Santa Monica. She asked everybody to come in The Spirit of Seventy-Six so we decided to come [dressed in this theme but] as the Marx Brothers. We went down to Western Costumes and rented the uniforms and the equipment. While we were rehearsing at the house, I placed the camera on a piano [and took this picture]. We rehearsed and decided how we were going to make our entrance. All the time we were rehearsing, we'd . . . stop in front of something and I'd say, as Harpo did, 'I chase blondes!'

"[It was late] when we got there and there were lots of people. The butler came and we said, 'Don't announce that we're here.' We then walked around, playing the drums and the fife. I saw this blonde so I just dropped the drumsticks and went and wrestled the blonde to the floor. [When I got back to playing] Fonda leaned over to me and said, 'Well you dumb son-of-a-bitch, that was Marion Davies!' "[14] The trio won second prize for their costumes. Marion Davies awarded the first prize to Mr. Hearst, her partner.

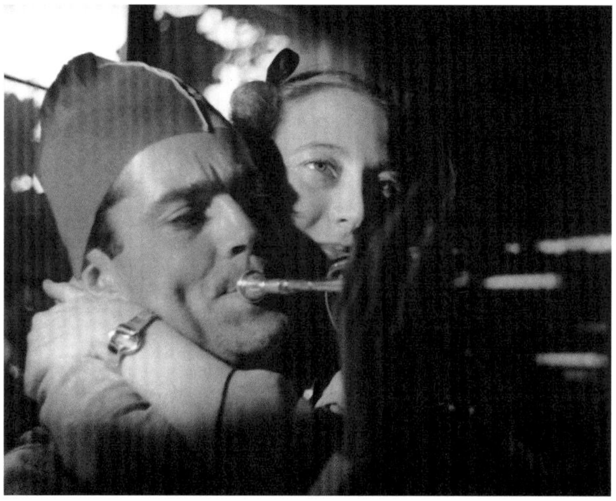

Henry and Frances Fonda, 1936

In the two years that Swope worked on the images for *Camera Over Hollywood*, he did not have his own darkroom but prevailed upon the generosity of his friend Peter Stackpole, who lived in a large house in Santa Monica Canyon. "I guess we thought of John in those days as being a jovial bachelor-about-town, coming from a prominent family, who seems to know all the big people of Hollywood socially without a hint that it ever affected the simplicity of life that he had chosen for himself. He'd drive a weather beaten old convertible and arrive wearing old clothes. If he'd arranged to use the darkroom he'd be in there for hours on end until the phone rang for him. I'd have to call him, then suddenly the darkroom door burst open and John would shout down the hall 'Hello, who is it?' so loudly that it would cause the person on the other end to start speaking before he reached the phone."[15]

• • •

When it came out in 1939, *Camera Over Hollywood* had ninety-six photographs in four groups: "Introduction to Glamour," "Extra Extra," "The Studio—A World in Itself," and "The Paths of Glory. . ." This was Swope's seemingly awkward categorization of his pictures according to different elements of filmmaking. Like Garry Winogrand after him, picture editing, sequencing, and layout were perhaps not Swope's primary skills. As Charles Poore noted in his review of *Camera Over Hollywood* in the *New York Times,* February 3, 1939, "The problem of designing a book that will hold together in a coherent pattern dozens of pictures of different sizes, by the way, seems to be as hard as ever to solve. There are still jarring discrepancies in the white spaces and the margins as one turns the pages."[16] Most of the photographs are reproduced on the right page of a spread, with short captions only on the left page. However, there may be more here than was evident to Poore. Today we are reminded of Walker Evans' *American Photographs* (1938), with its blank left-hand pages.

Bennett Cerf's agreement to publish Swope's book at Random House was conditional upon the usual controls of the Random House editorial board. In correspondence Cerf suggested that Swope include more "personality pictures"—meaning stars—to give the book broad, glamorous appeal. Internal evidence suggests that Swope ignored this direction. Swope also ignored deadlines. "Your indignant constituency would like to know when the hell it or they are going to see the pictures for whose taking you permanently disrupted the appearance of this office. They respectfully suggest that you cease molesting Miss Edey long enough to develop these pictures and bring them around here. Or else . . . Indignantly, Bennett Cerf."[17]

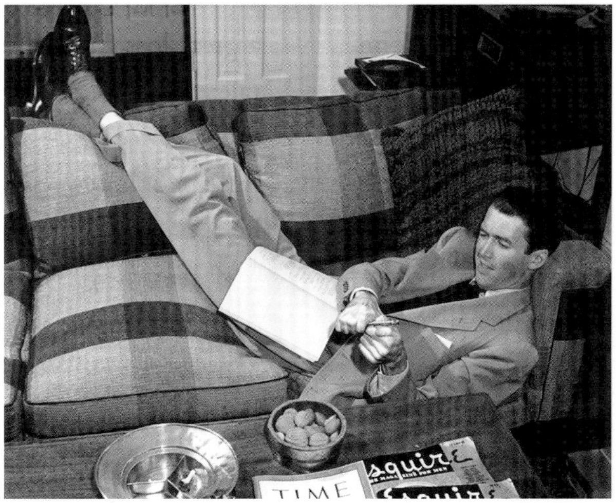

Jimmy Stewart on couch cracking walnuts, 1938

Copies of *Camera Over Hollywood* were sent out Christmas of 1939 to a virtual Who's Who of the world of entertainment and power. Swope kept some of the letters and telegrams sent in thanks. "You really should have a perfect Christmas after the publication of your really magnificent book. Congratulations dear Johnny on your frantic head and love, The Duchess."[18]

When he finished *Camera Over Hollywood* Swope knew he had done something important. It contradicted commonly held assumptions about Hollywood and challenged photographic conventions. The idealized vision of Hollywood photographers such as George Hurrell and Clarence Sinclair Bull was nowhere to be seen in Swope's work. But equally, Swope was not a photojournalist or social documentarian. His achievement, in the heyday of *LIFE* magazine, the Farm Security Administration, and high modernist cinema star photography, was to make pictures that were intelligent and graceful and transparently observant of a fantasy-driven culture.

• • •

Swope's career was just beginning, but his character and style were already fully formed. As Peter Stackpole noted, "Once you got to know Swope you learned to expect the unexpected. Something was bound to happen causing some consternation, but you never knew what or when. He'd take my wife flying at the Santa Monica airfield and ask her to let him know if she saw any planes getting too close. What was he supposed to be doing? [Later] At Thunderbird Field in Arizona during the war, Swope was instructing Chinese students in basic flying. I took a flight with John in order to photograph a student in another plane. When we finished [the shoot] John put the trainer into a graceful falling leaf rhythm while he sang a Strauss Waltz through the mike."[19]

After his heady few years in Hollywood, Swope

and Josh Logan set out on an extensive tour of South America, from Panama to Tierra del Fuego. After he returned to the United States, Swope was attending a party at Leland Hayward's Bel Air home, where he met actress Dorothy McGuire,[20] then under contract to David O. Selznick. As Henry Fonda recounted, "About four years later I returned to my home in Omaha and played the Policeman in Sir James Barrie's *A Kiss for Cinderella* at the Omaha Community Playhouse where I had spawned some years before. My Cinderella was a lovely, almost frighteningly talented thirteen-year-old named Dorothy McGuire who has gone on to become her own legend. Somehow, with no help from me, John and Dorothy met, made sparks, and married while I was off somewhere, and they remain today my closest and dearest friends."[21]

When the United States joined the war, Swope was recruited by Edward Steichen to be one of his photographers stationed on an aircraft carrier to document the war in the Pacific. As the first photographer to land ashore in Japan just prior to the signing of the declaration of surrender, Swope was able to spend three weeks photographing a devastated country whose people were about to face the realities of rebuilding an entirely new economy and society.

After the war Peter Stackpole remembered, "I felt that John had the taste and class to have become an important film maker, but more and more it became obvious that his creative juices needed his camera and his darkroom and that's where he was happiest. His work began to be accepted by important national magazines and within a very short time he became a regular contributor to *LIFE* magazine. His first cover was a spectacular full head portrait of his daughter, Topo, at the age of forty-five minutes."[22]

In the early to mid-1950s, John and Dorothy McGuire both played important roles in Southern California's legitimate theater at the La Jolla Playhouse, just south of Los Angeles. As with the University Players Group that had so inspired Swope's first love of theater, he was similarly engaged to serve as both producer and company photographer.

Film producer Norman Lloyd recollects that at this time Swope was "as tasteful and knowledgeable a producer as I have ever encountered. I cannot remember ever disagreeing with his discerning observations. And, with his superb eye, he knew much about staging and, of course, lighting. I trusted his taste implicitly. It was a great loss that John did not pursue this aspect of his talent. John, I believe, selected the freedom of photography where he could do his work without interference. In his noble way, he was the most sensitive of men. For him, there was more to be achieved in roaming the world with his camera and seeing 'the family of man' than arguing a story point in some studio office. Fortunately, he had the means to remain a 'loner' and the art of photography is all the better for it."[23]

• • •

After Swope's death in 1979, Henry Fonda found his way of explaining to a bereaved Dorothy McGuire some of the qualities that made Swope special to him: "I loved John. I truly did. I was just 23 when we first became friends and I don't think I originally appreciated how much his outgoing, giving, resounding personality affected me in a positive way. But it wasn't long before I recognized that he was truly unique. And what an experience. What a pleasure it was for me to be in his company. I have never known a man to so thoroughly enjoy life as John did and to live it as fully. His enthusiasms were contagious. You always felt better for having been with John."[24]

Notes

1. Leland Hayward. Introduction to *Camera Over Hollywood,* Random House, 1939.

2. Leland Hayward. Original and unedited introduction to *Camera Over Hollywood,* Random House, 1939. The John Swope Archive, Los Angeles.

3. *Hollywood: Mecca of the Movies,* Blaise Cendrars, with 29 drawings from life by Jean Guérin, translated and introduced by Garrett White. University of California Press, 1995.

4, 5. *Ibid.*

6. Donald Dewey, from *James Stewart: A Biography,* Turner Publishing, Inc., 1996. Dewey goes on to add, "Other important members of the troupe were Myron McCormick, who would alternate steady work on Broadway with key supporting roles in the movies, such as Andy Griffith's tormented sergeant on *No Time For Sergeants* and Paul Newman's friend in *The Hustler;* Barbara O'Neil, who won screen attention as the mother of Scarlett O'Hara in *Gone With the Wind* and Best Supporting Actress Oscar nomination for the 1940 soap opera *All This and Heaven Too;* Mildred Natwick, who would make a career of portraying comical, eccentric mothers, most notably in *Barefoot in the Park* and in the television series *McMillan and Wife;* and Josh Logan, who would end up shuttling between Broadway and Hollywood most of his life; Harvard premed student and future doctor, Bart Quigley, whose most lasting contribution to the theater would be his daughter, actress and National Endowment for the Arts chief, Jane Alexander."

   Among others in the University Players were Margaret Sullavan, Charles Crane Leatherbee, Bretaigne Windlust, Merna Pace, Cynthia Rogers, and Kent Smith.

7. Henry Fonda, February 1979. From his preface written for a retrospective book of Swope's photographs—not published. The John Swope Archive, Los Angeles.

8. Jane Alexander in *James Stewart: A Biography.* Donald Dewey. Turner Publishing, Inc., 1996.

9. *Ibid.*

10. (unpublished and undated notes by Robert Strauss, circa 1979) The John Swope Archive, Los Angeles.

11. Leland Hayward. Original and unedited introduction to *Camera Over Hollywood,* Random House, 1939. The John Swope Archive, Los Angeles.

12. From an unpublished essay by Peter Stackpole, circa 1979. The John Swope Archive, Los Angeles.

13. Henry Fonda, February 1979. From his preface written for a retrospective book of Swope's photographs—not published. The John Swope Archive, Los Angeles.

14. Unpublished transcript of an interview by John Swope, circa 1976. The John Swope Archive, Los Angeles.

15. From an unpublished essay by Peter Stackpole, circa 1979. The John Swope Archive, Los Angeles.

16. Charles Poore, *The New York Times,* February 3, 1939.

17. Letter to John Swope from Bennett Cerf, Random House, January 10, 1939. The John Swope Archive, Los Angeles.

18. The Duchess of York, Western Union Cable to John Swope, December 23, 1939. The John Swope Archive, Los Angeles.

19. From an unpublished essay by Peter Stackpole, circa 1979. The John Swope Archive, Los Angeles.

20. Dorothy McGuire's film roles at the time included *Claudia,* 1943; *A Tree Grows in Brooklyn* and *Enchanted Cottage,* 1945; and *Gentleman's Agreement,* 1947.

21. *Ibid.,* 13.

22. *Ibid.,* 16.

23. *The La Jolla Years with John Swope: 1953-54-55.* Norman Lloyd, circa 1979. The John Swope Archive, Los Angeles. Also from an interview with Norman Lloyd by Graham Howe and Mark Swope, December 5, 1998.

24. Letter to Dorothy McGuire, July 1979. *Fonda: My Life.* As told to Howard Teichmann, New American Library Books, Times Mirror, 1981. Page 339.

Chronology: John Swope, American, 1908–1979

1908	Born August 23 in New Brunswick, New Jersey.
1926	Attends Harvard University.
1927	Joins University Players theater group with Henry Fonda, Josh Logan, and James Stewart.
1930	Graduates from Harvard University.
1930–1931	Travels to Japan, Korea, China, India, Italy, Germany, and England.
1933–1936	Works for the National Recovery Administration, Washington, D.C., and later for the Resettlement Administration.
1939	*Camera Over Hollywood* is published by Random House. First solo exhibition at Carroll Carstairs Gallery, New York.
1939	Travels to South America with Josh Logan on assignment for *Harper's Bazaar*.
1940–1943	Works as flying instructor for the United States Air Force at Thunderbird Field, Arizona.
1942	Collaborates with John Steinbeck on a military commission to produce a book about the Navy's pilot training program.
1943	*Bombs Away* is published by Viking Press, New York. Text by John Steinbeck, photographs by John Swope.
1943	Marries actress Dorothy McGuire.
1943–1945	Assigned to Edward Steichen's special photographic unit for the United States Navy, and documents release of POWs at the end of the war in Japan.
1945–1959	Freelance photographer for *LIFE* magazine.
1948	Travels to Europe.
1949	Daughter Topo is born February 14.
1950	Travels to India, Bali, Japan, and Israel.

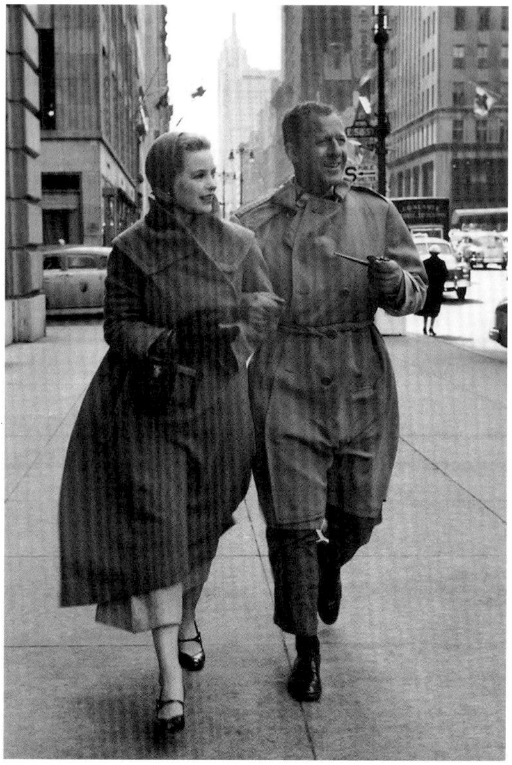

Dorothy McGuire and John Swope in New York, 1943

1952	Solo exhibition at Albright-Knox Art Gallery, Buffalo, New York.
1952–1957	Producer at the La Jolla Playhouse in California.
1953	Son Mark is born May 14.
	Solo exhibition at the Santa Barbara Art Museum, California.
1956	Two-person exhibition by John Swope and John Szarkowski at the Nelson Atkins Museum, Kansas City, Missouri.
1958–1978	Extensive travels to Europe, Russia, Africa, India, South and Central America, China, Japan, Australia, and New Zealand.
1961	Solo exhibition at the Phoenix Art Museum, Arizona.
1962	Solo exhibition at the Art Museum, Princeton University, New Jersey.
1963	Solo exhibition at the Joslyn Art Museum, Omaha, Nebraska.
1967	Photographic study of Jacques Lipchitz, University of California at Los Angeles.
1973	Photographs the sculptural installation *Henry Moore in America,* curated by Henry J. Seldis at the Los Angeles County Museum of Art.
1975	*Autobiography of a Princess,* compiled by James Ivory, screenplay by Ruth Prawer Jhabvala, with photographs by John Swope, published by Harper and Row.
1978	Solo exhibition at the Art Garden, Venice, California.
1979	Dies at the age of seventy on May 11 in Los Angeles.
1987–1990	Group exhibition *Masters of Starlight,* at the Los Angeles County Museum of Art, California. Curated by David Fahey and Linda Rich.
	An abbreviated version of this exhibition traveled to the Parco Gallery, Tokyo, and the Pavilion Des Arts, Paris.
1992	Group exhibition *Hollywood Hollywood,* at Art Center College of Design, Pasadena, California.
1994–1998	Traveling group exhibition *Kissing,* curated by the G. Ray Hawkins Gallery, Los Angeles, California.
1996	Solo exhibition at the Craig Krull Gallery, Santa Monica, California.

Hollywood Boulevard, 1938

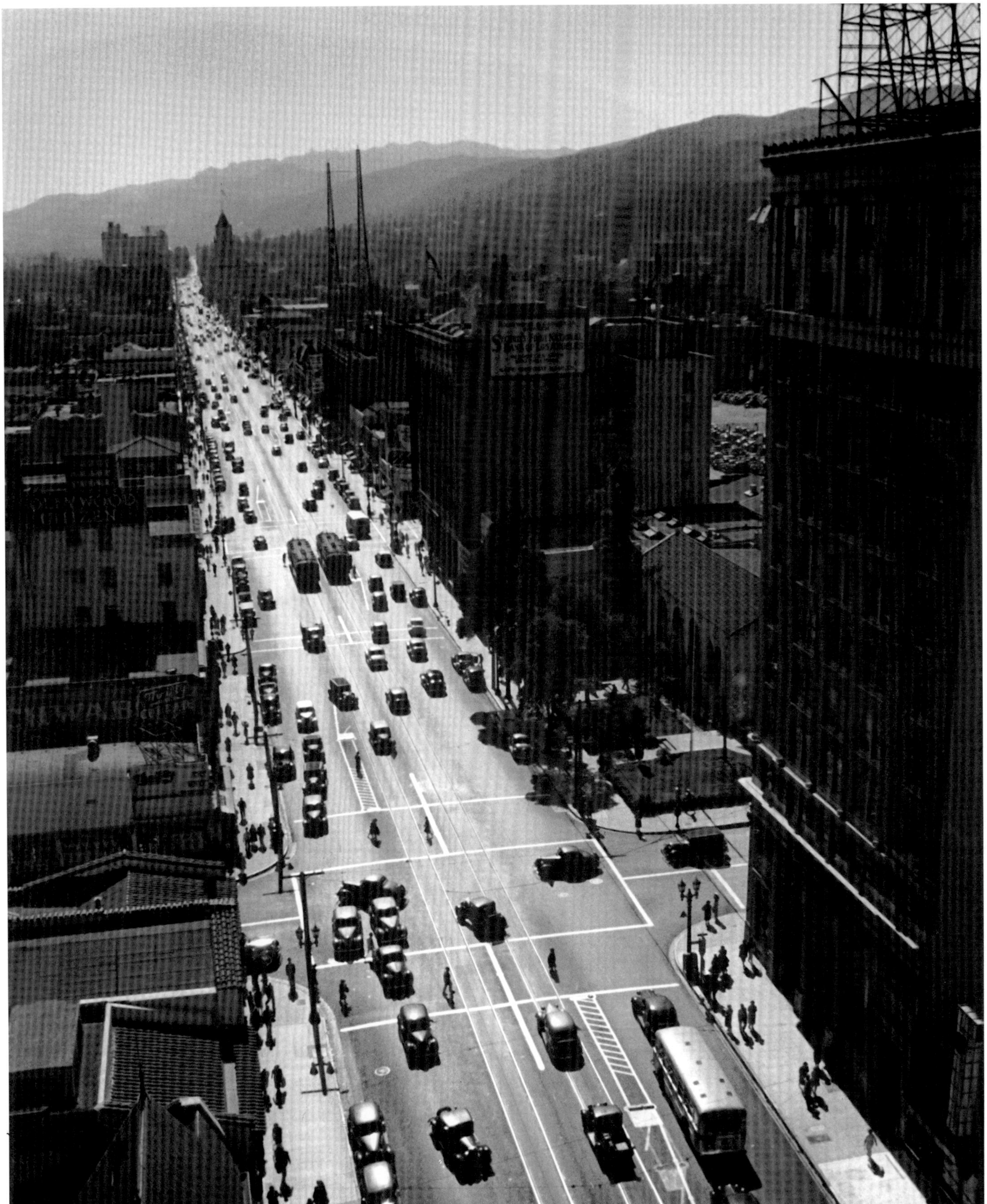

Woman with suitcase, Main Street, 1938

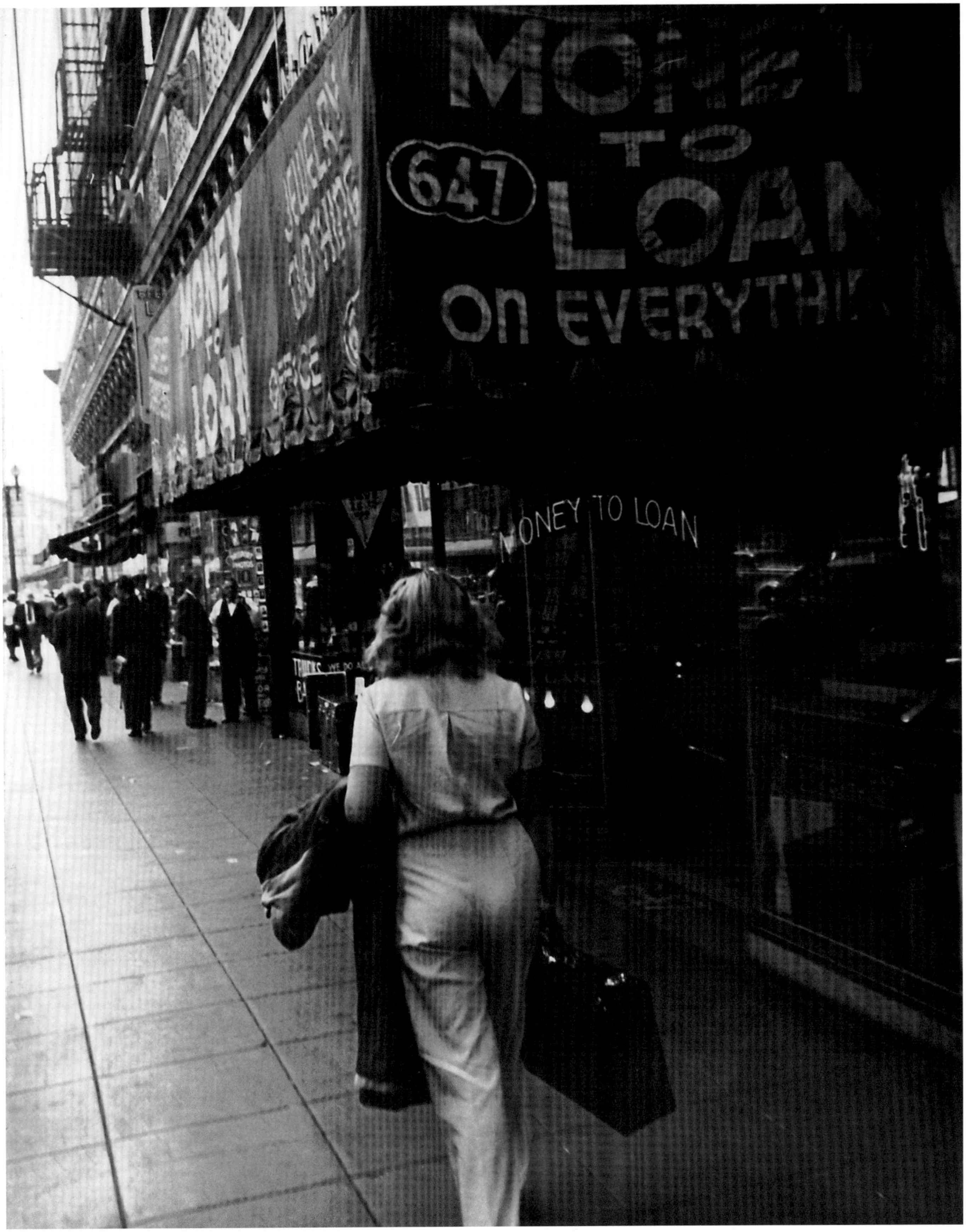
TO
647
LOAN
MONEY TO LOAN

"First Time on Main Street: *Stage Door,*" 1937

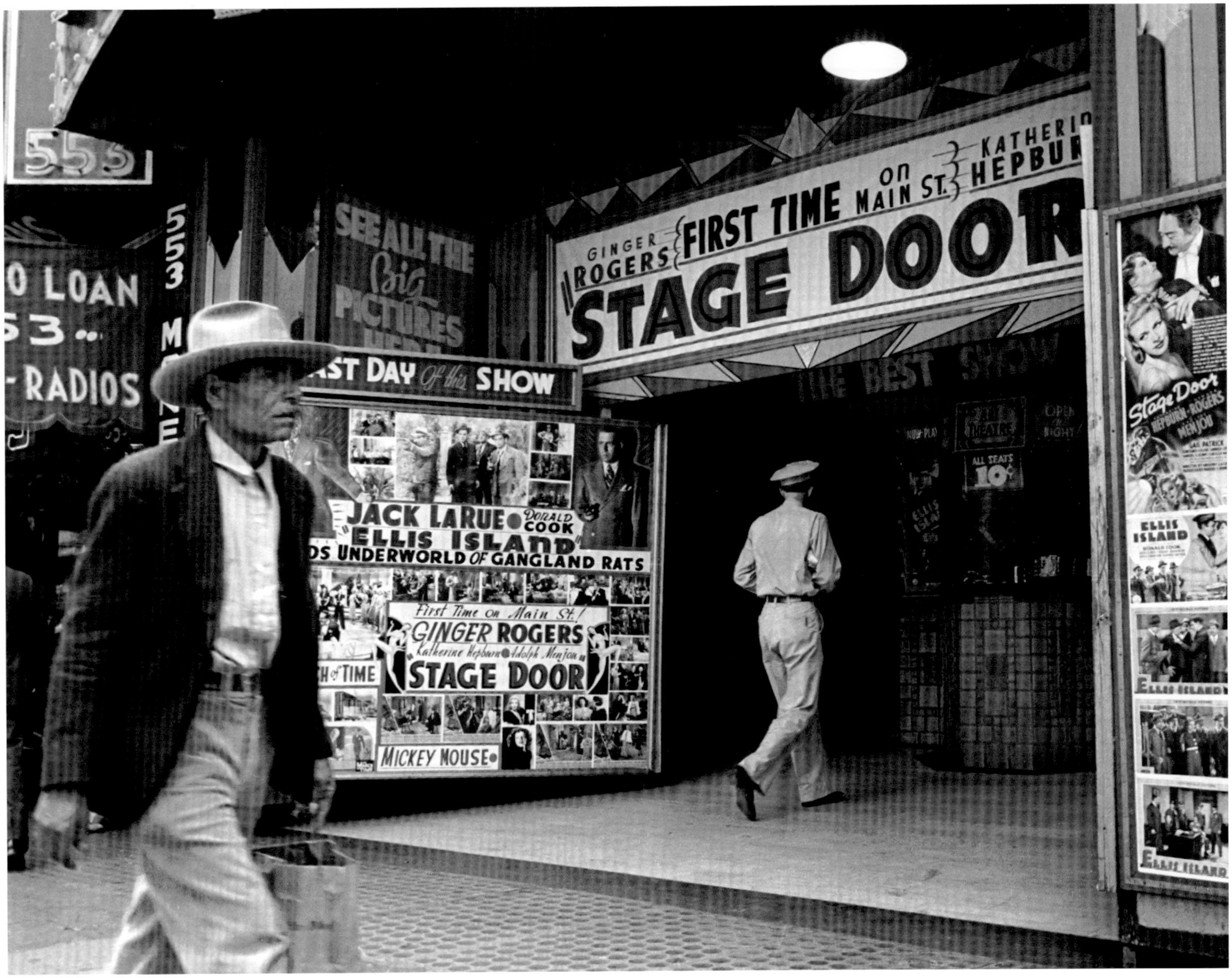
553
O LOAN
RADIOS
553
SEE ALL THE
Big
PICTURES
ST DAY Of this SHOW
GINGER ROGERS
FIRST TIME
ON MAIN ST.
KATHERIN
HEPBUR
STAGE DOOR
THE BEST SHOW
ALL SEATS 10¢
JACK LARUE
DONALD COOK
"ELLIS ISLAND"
DS UNDERWORLD OF GANGLAND RATS
First Time on Main St.!
GINGER ROGERS
Katherine Hepburn Adolph Menjou
STAGE DOOR
MICKEY MOUSE
Stage Door
HEPBURN ROGERS
MENJOU
ELLIS ISLAND

Sunset Boulevard at Sunset Plaza Drive, 1938

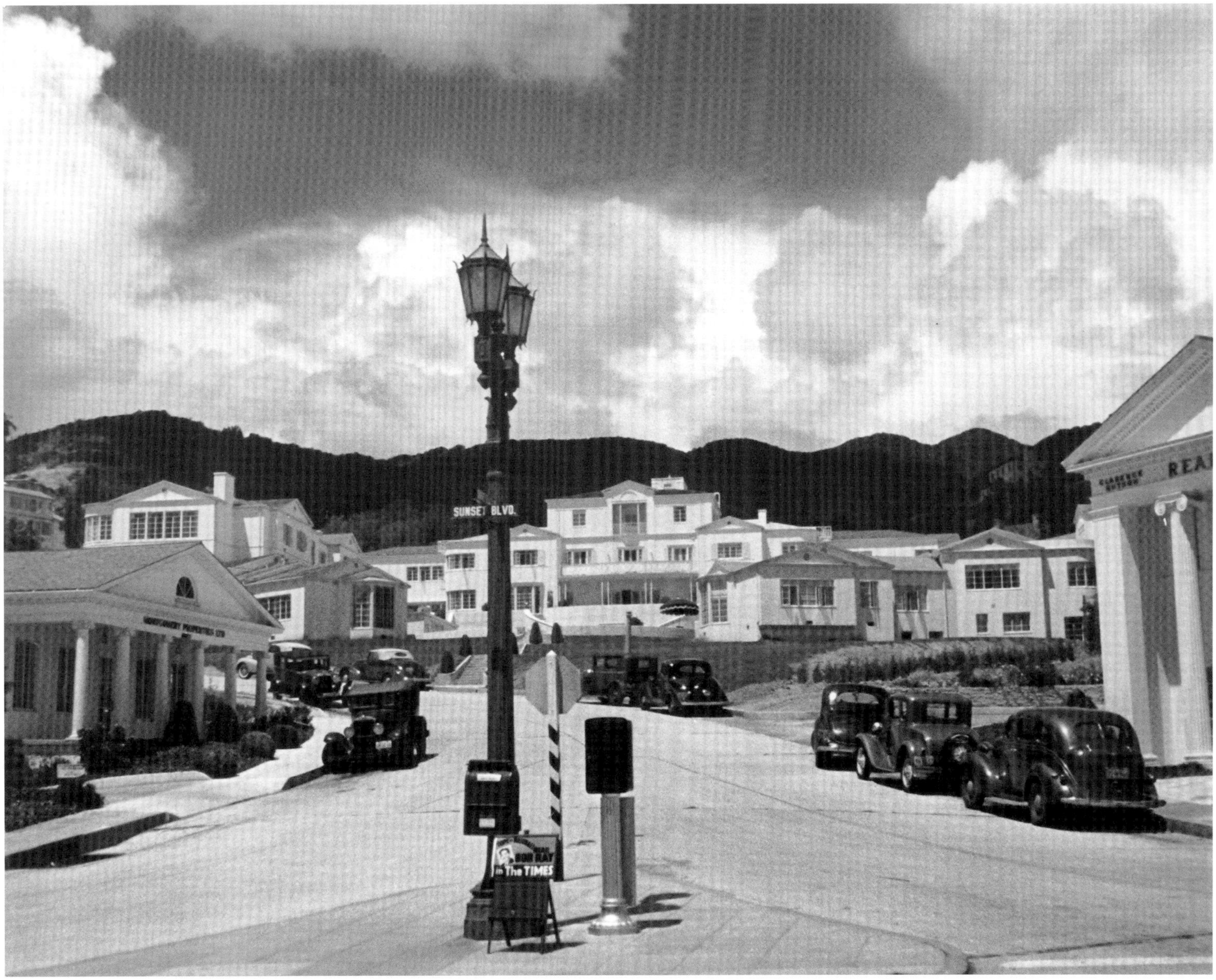
SUNSET BLVD.
in The TIMES

Two women entering Paramount Pictures studios, 1938

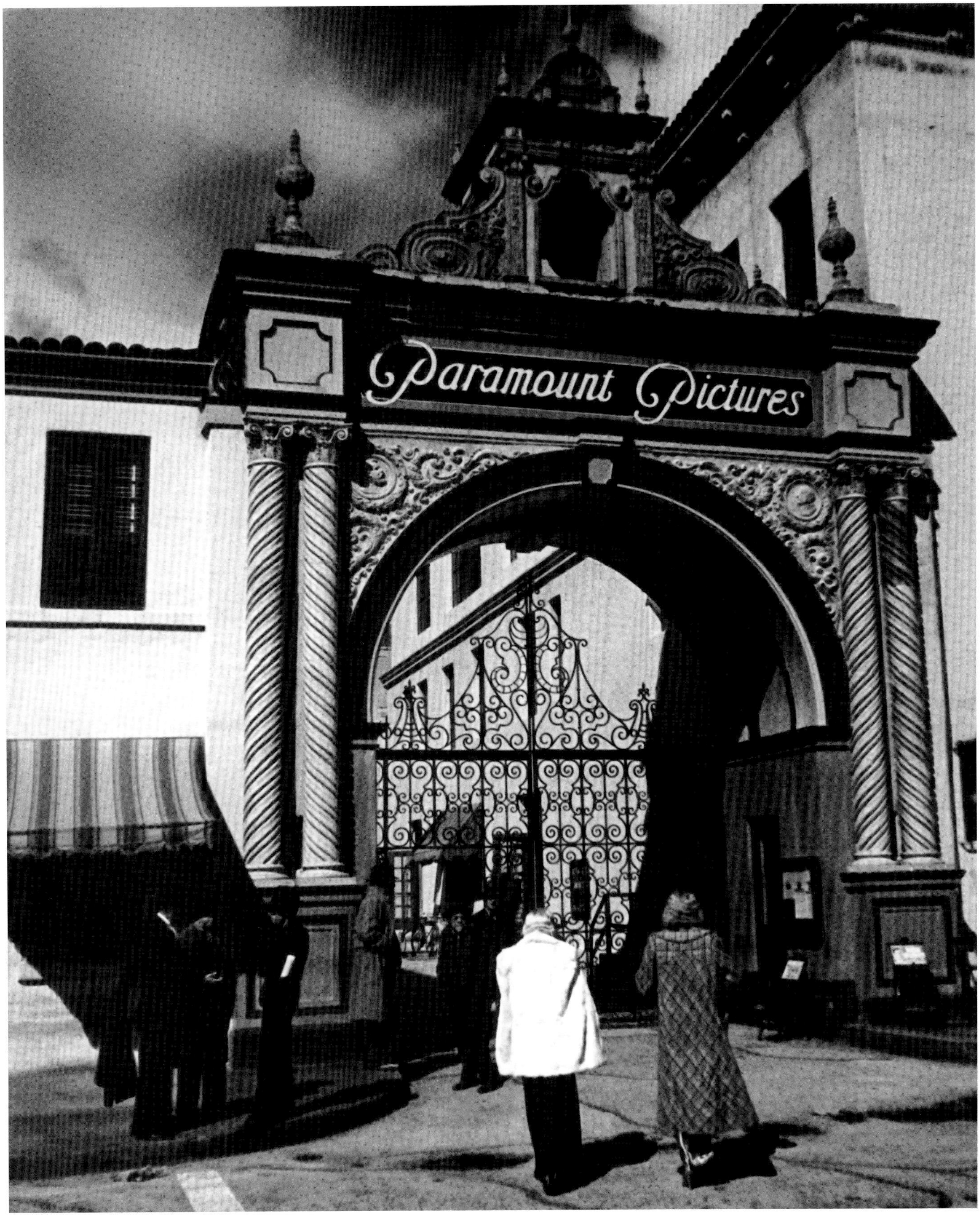
Paramount Pictures

Filming movie scene on back lot, 1938

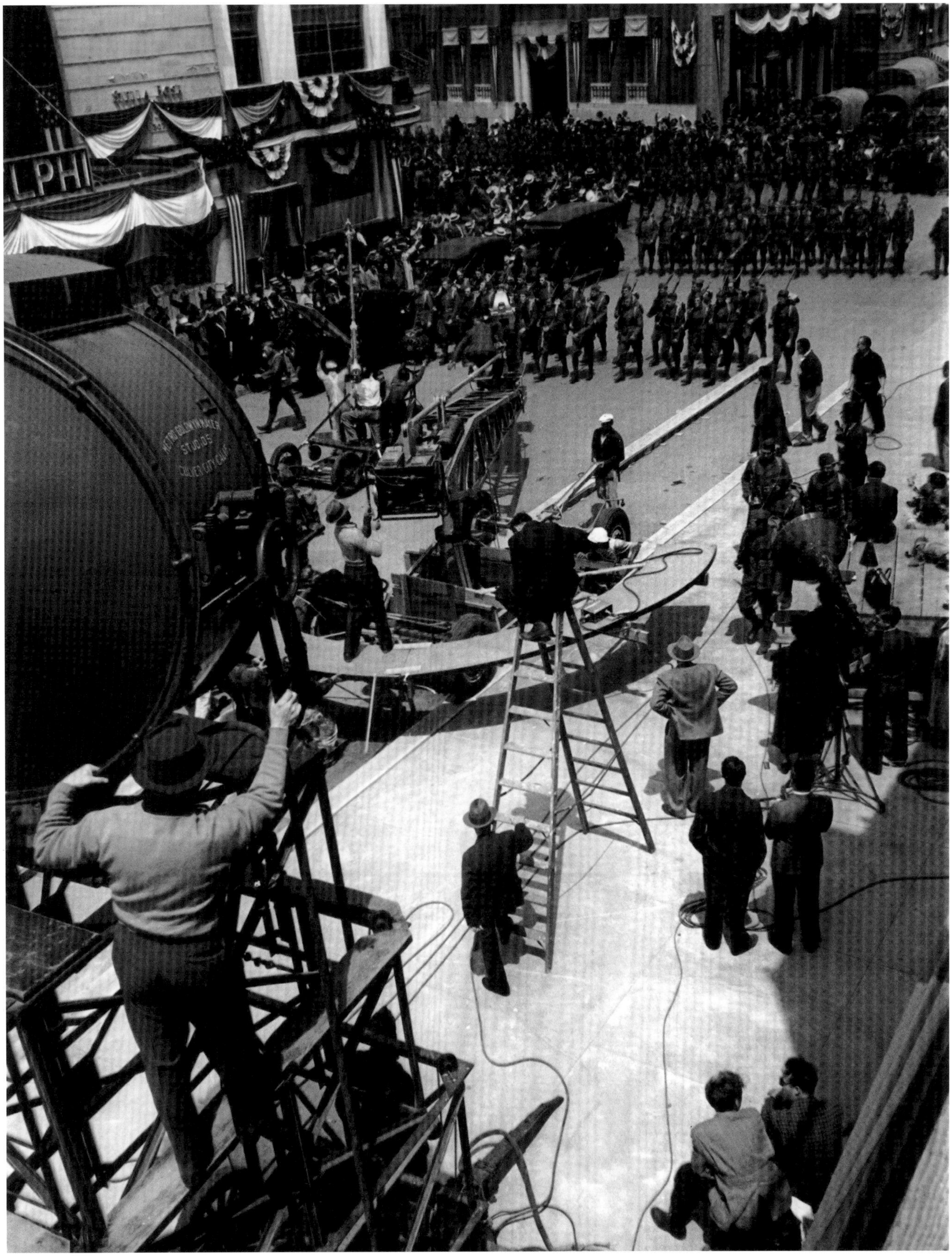
LPHI

MGM casting office, 1938

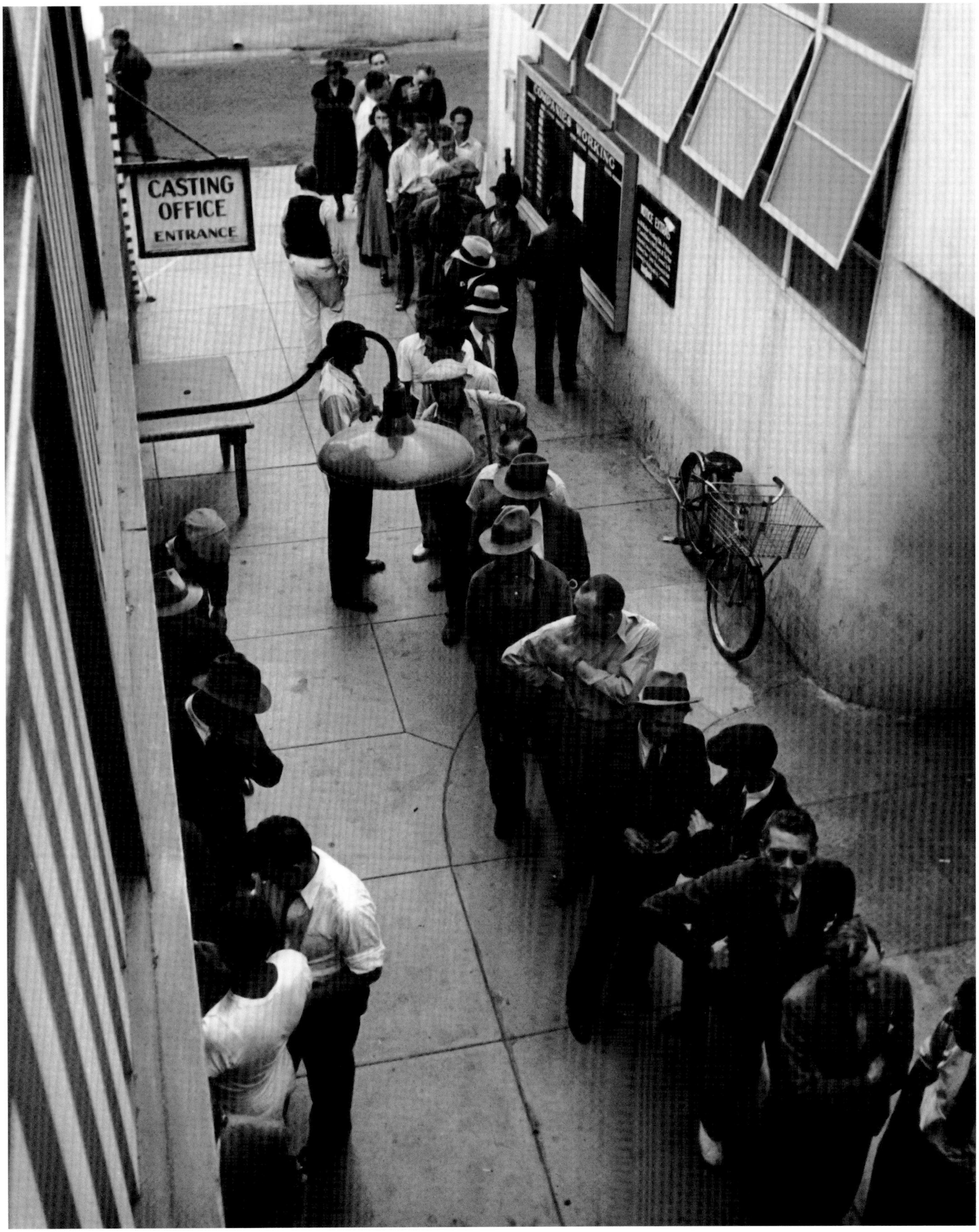
CASTING
OFFICE
ENTRANCE

Rosalind Russell with script of *The Citadel,* 1938

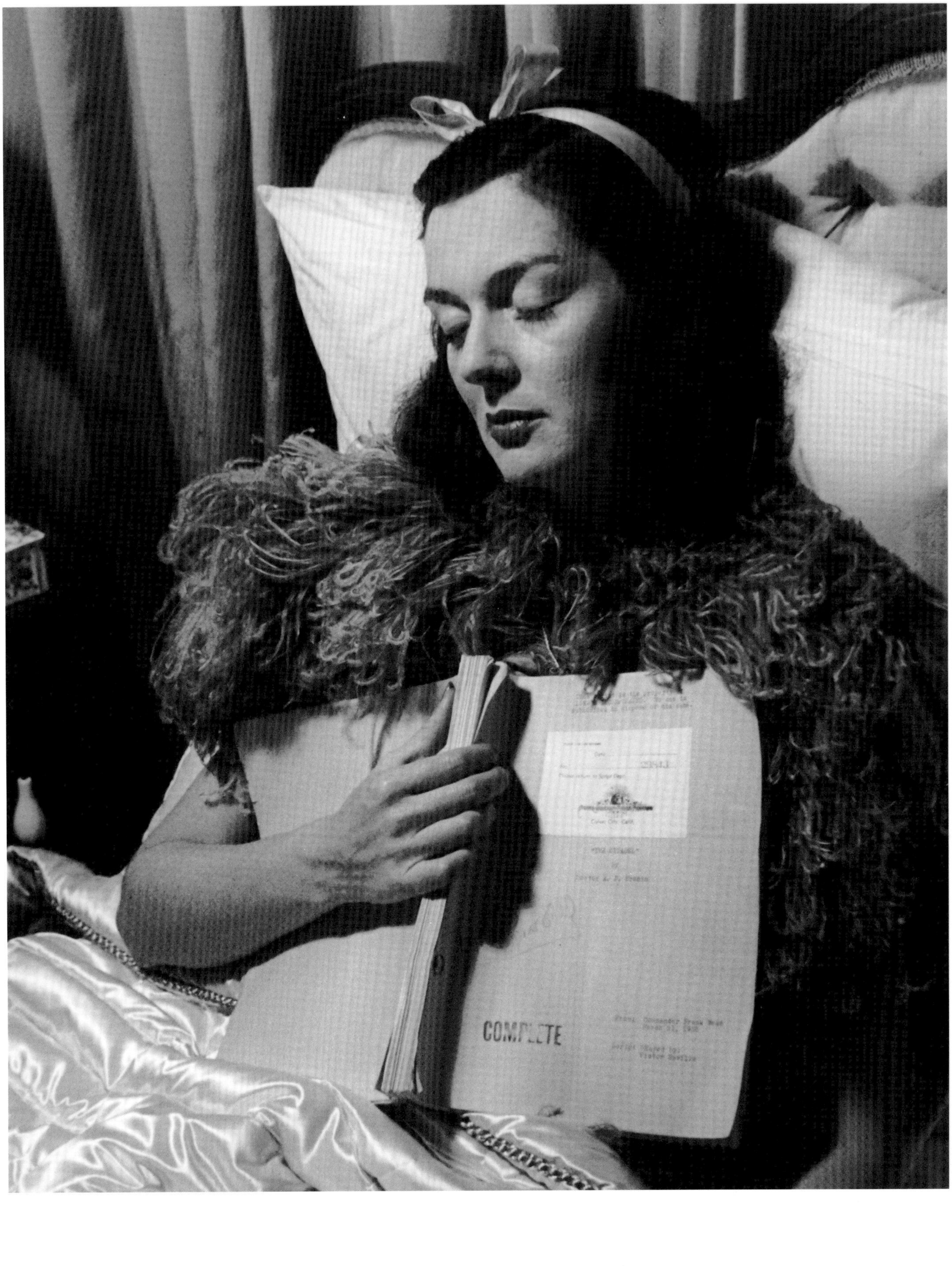
COMPLETE

Extras waiting backstage, 1938

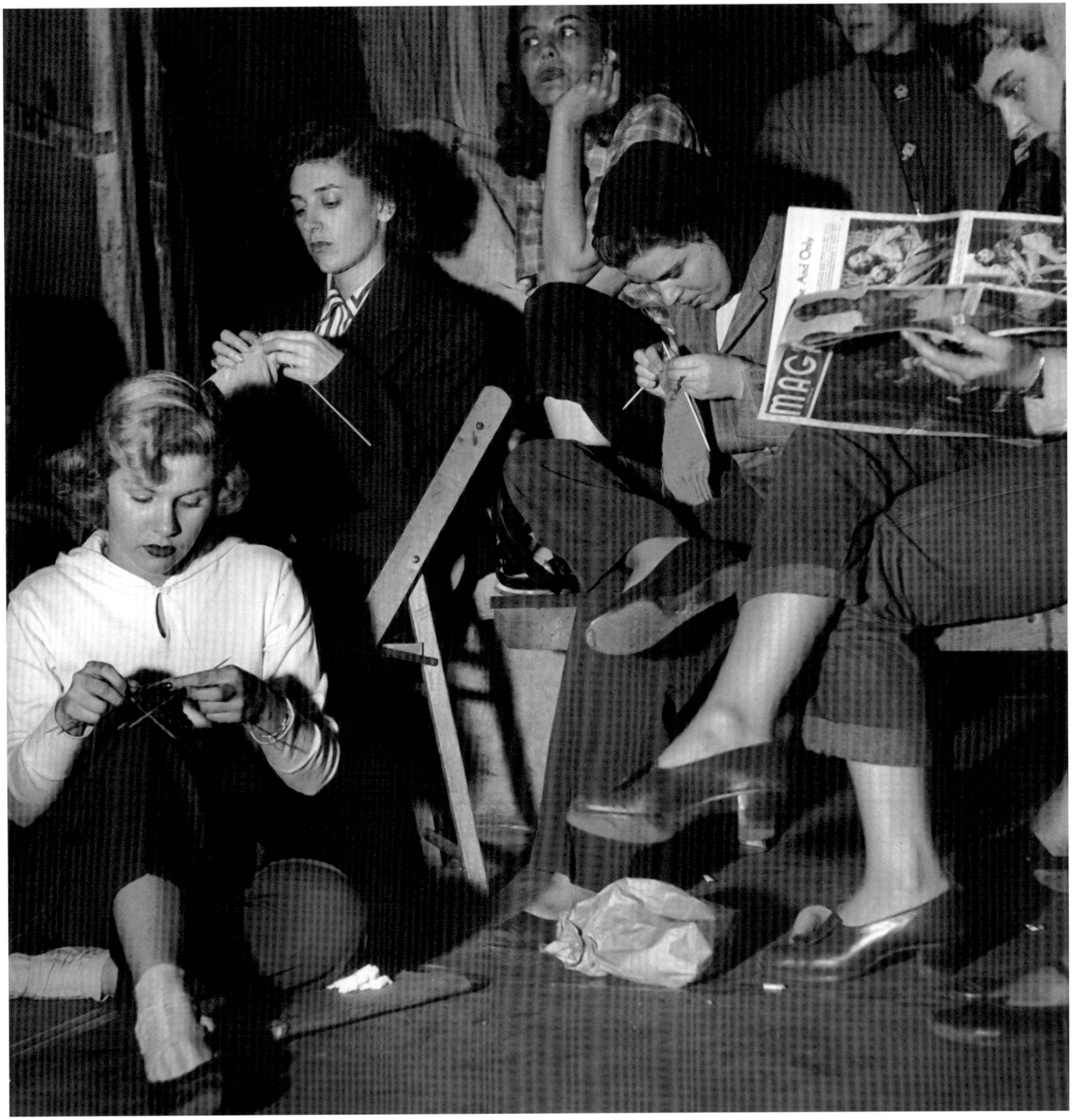

On a movie set, 1938

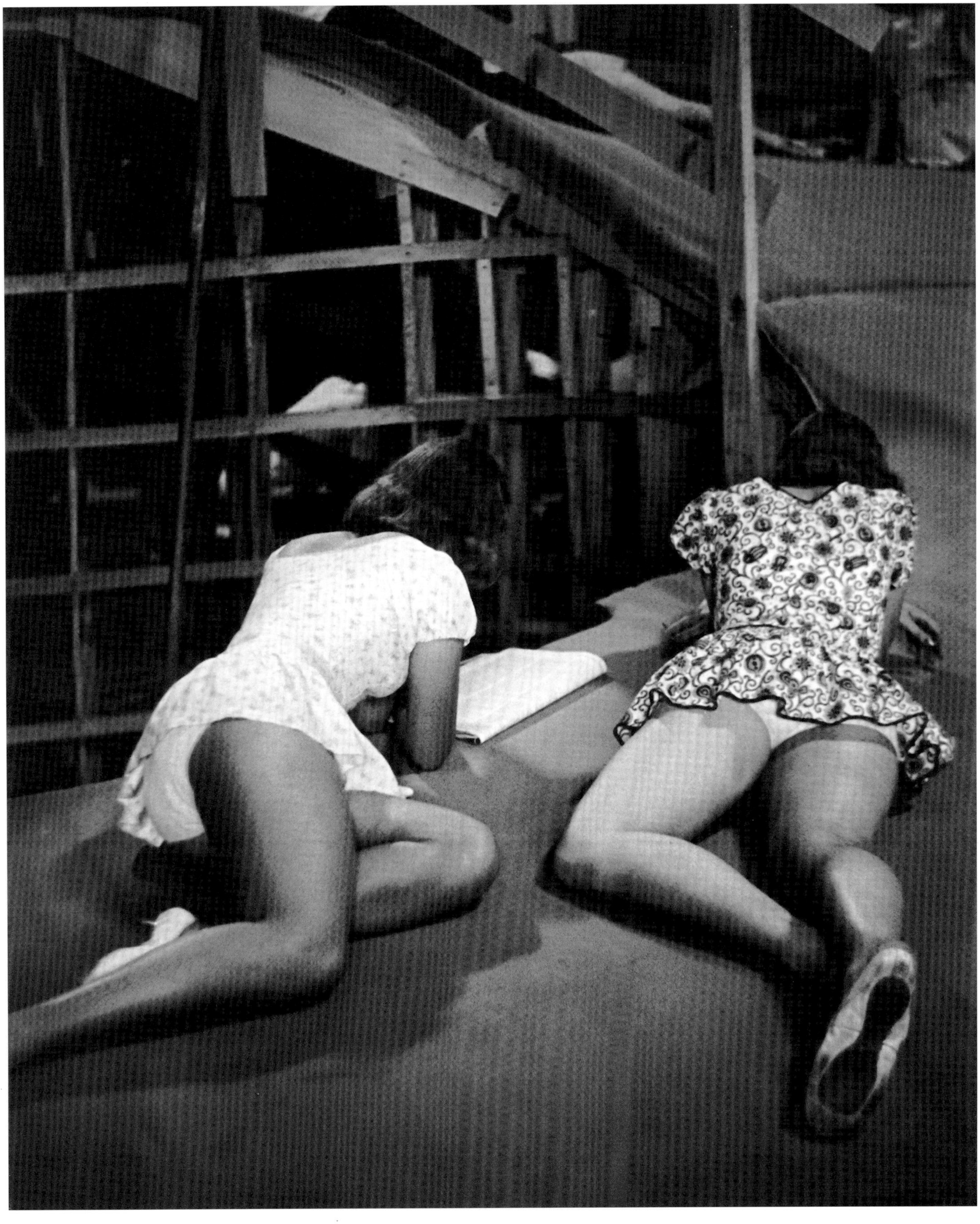

Sleeping extra, *Shopworn Angel,* 1938

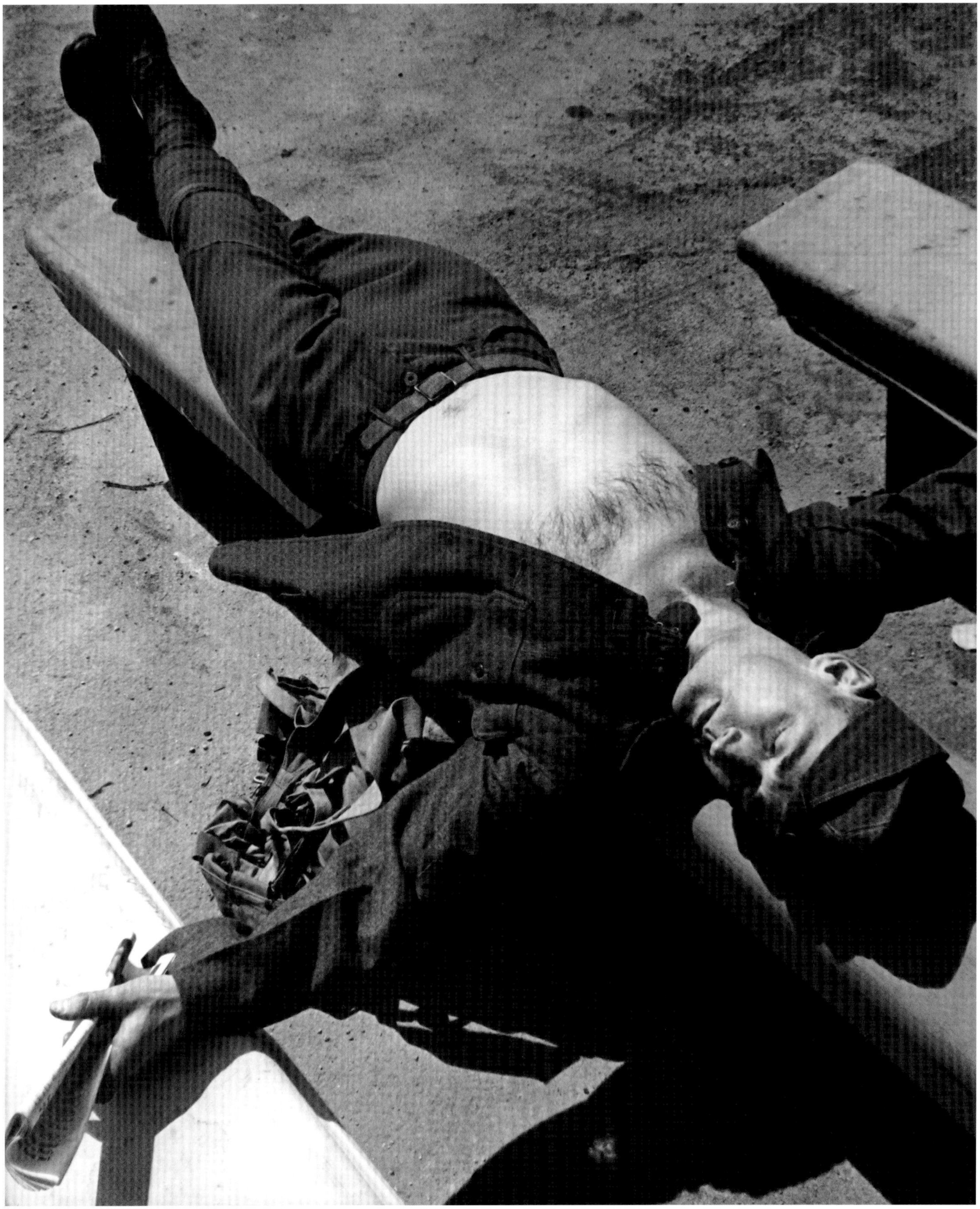

MGM prop shop, our Lady of Liberty, 1938

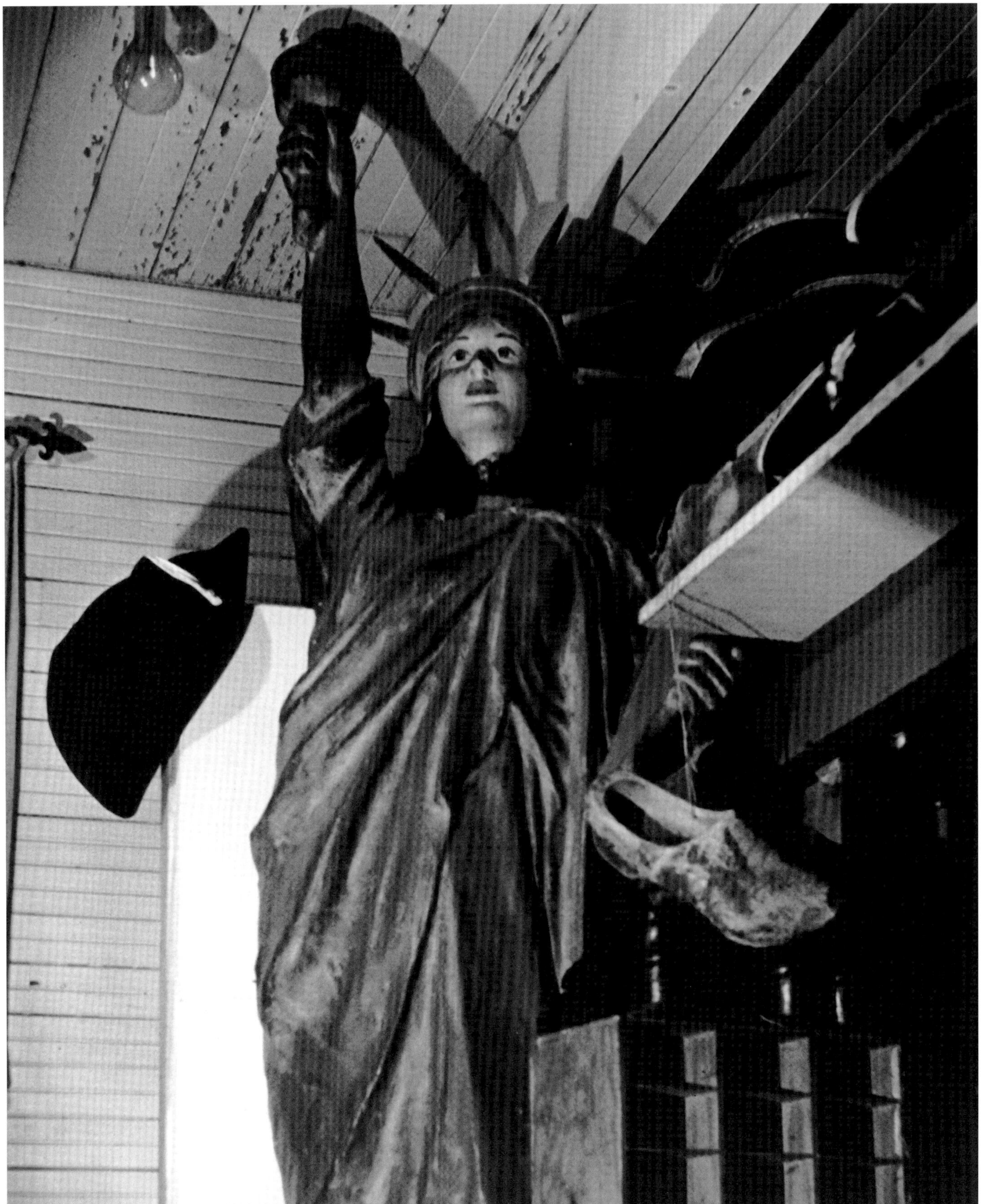

James Wong Howe with 35mm camera, 1938

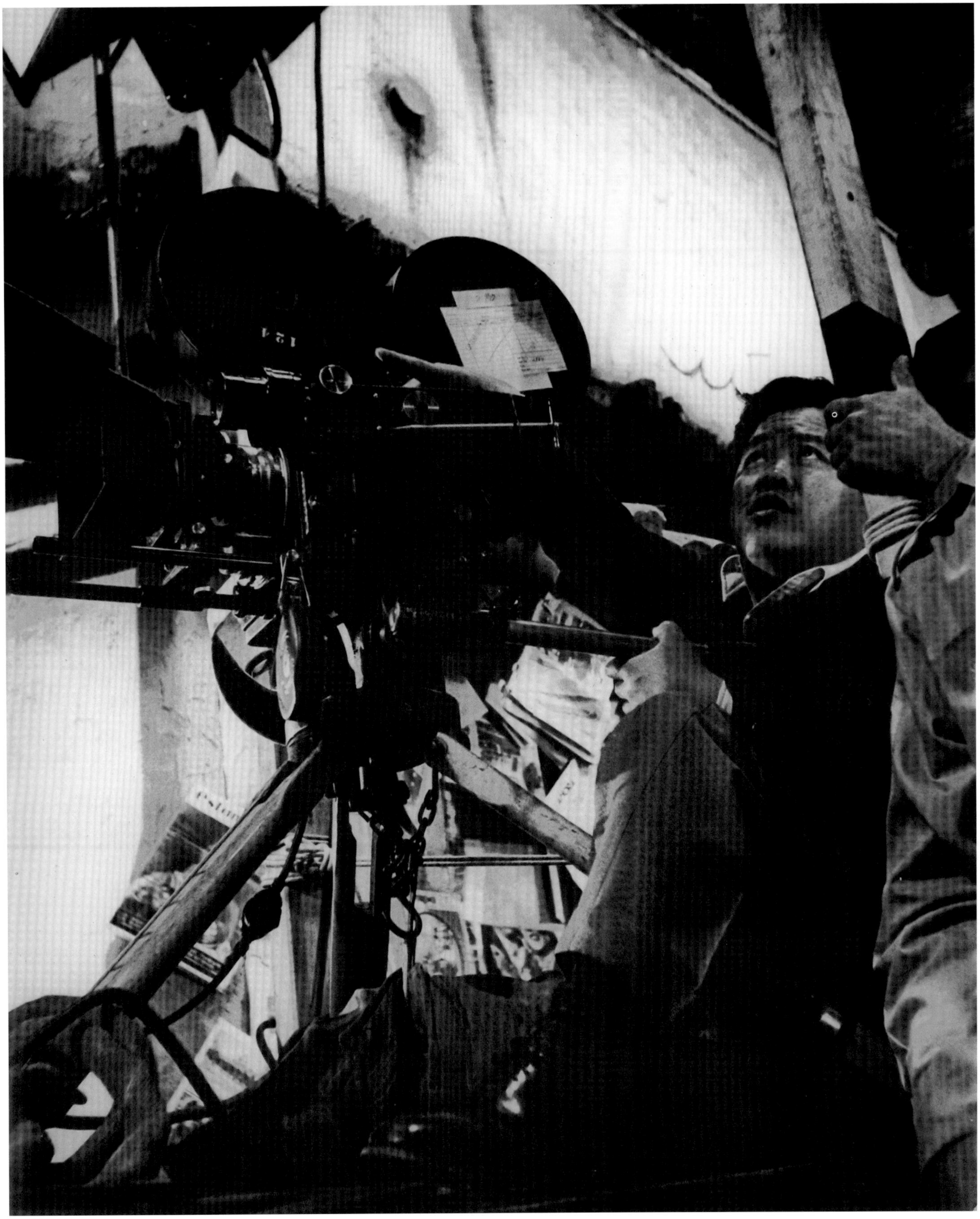

Wood scaffolding tower on movie set, 1938

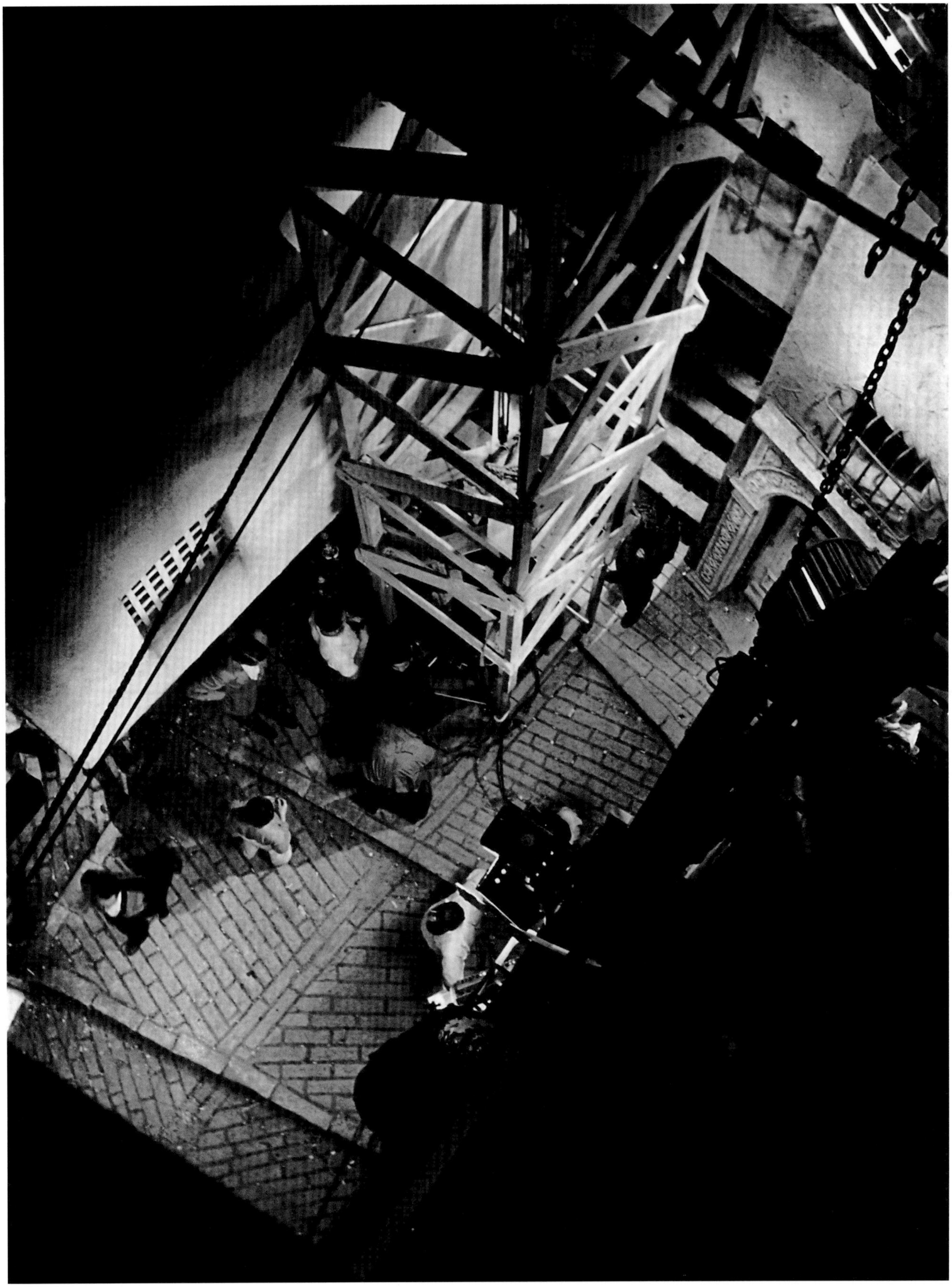

Stage lighting in winter set, 1938

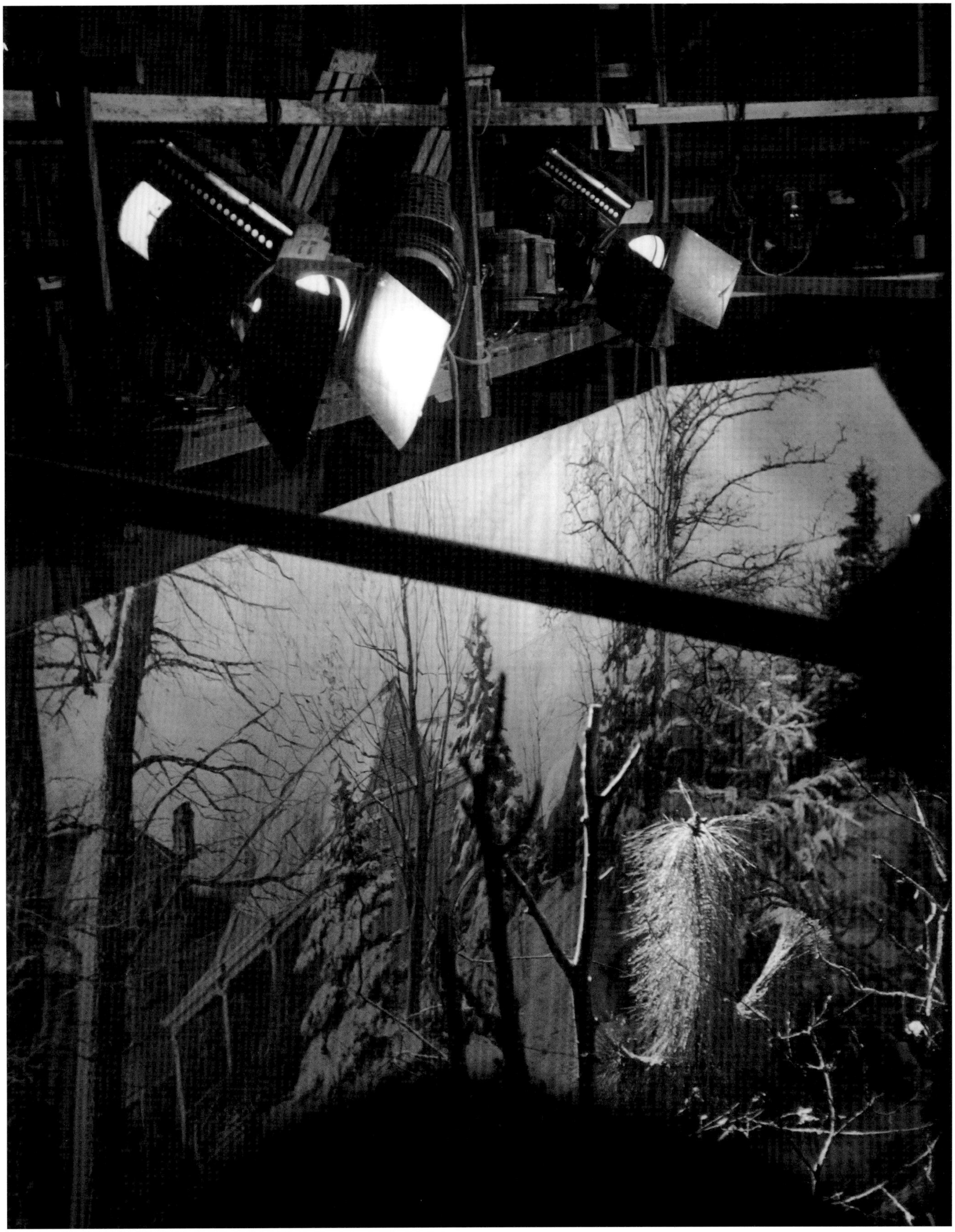

Building a city, studio back lot, 1937

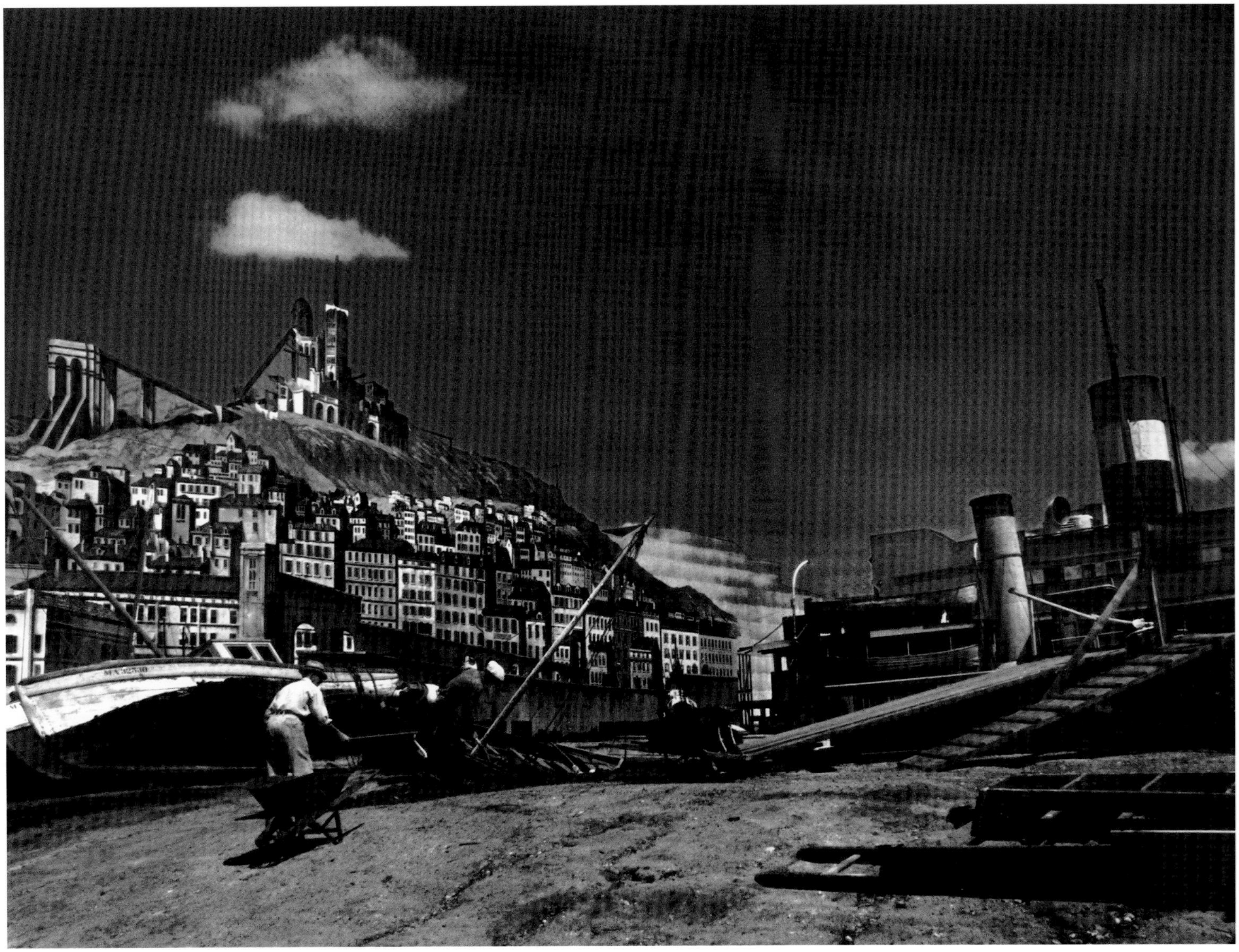

Charles Boyer in his dressing room, 1938

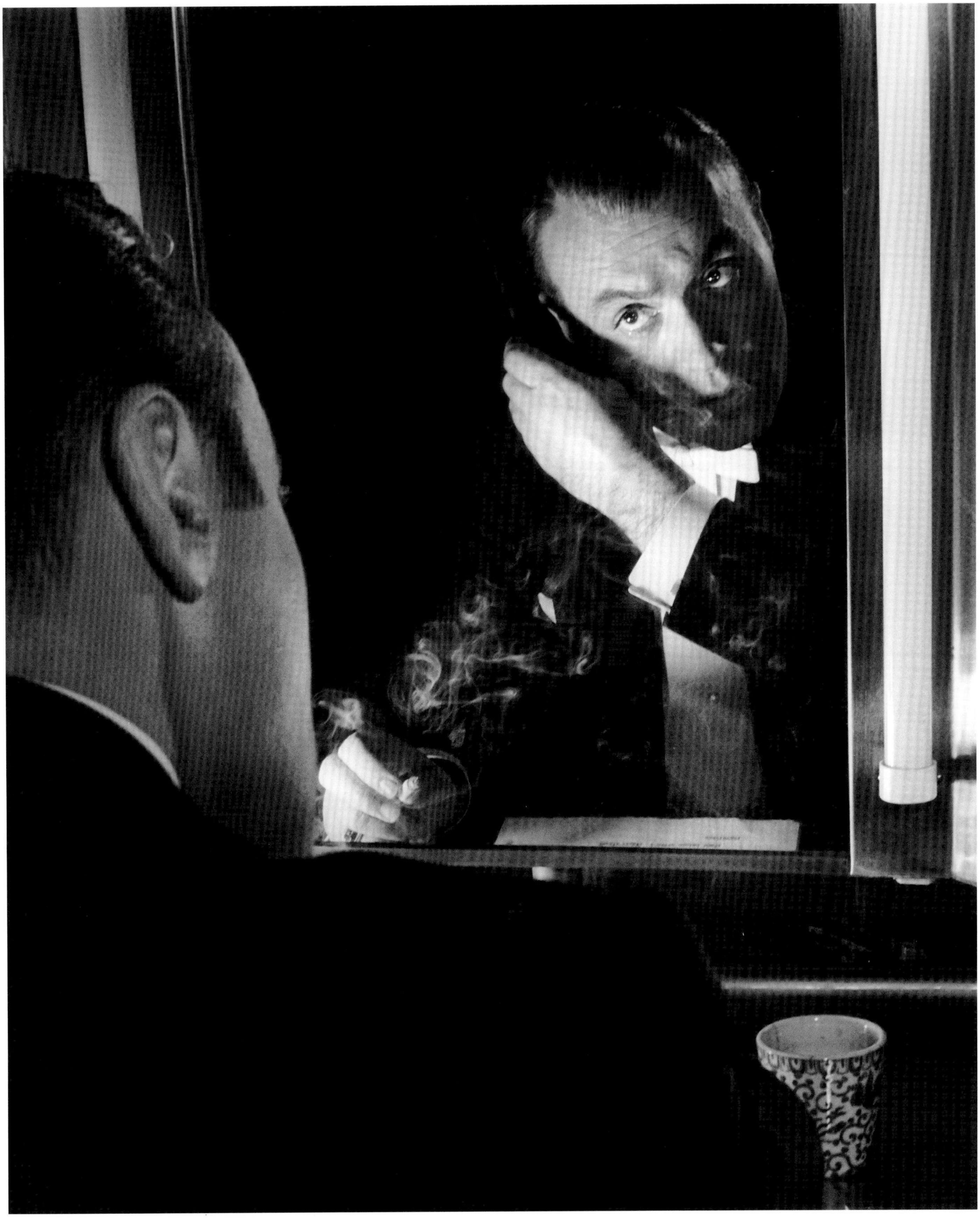

Test of Miss Whitney, take 4B, 1938

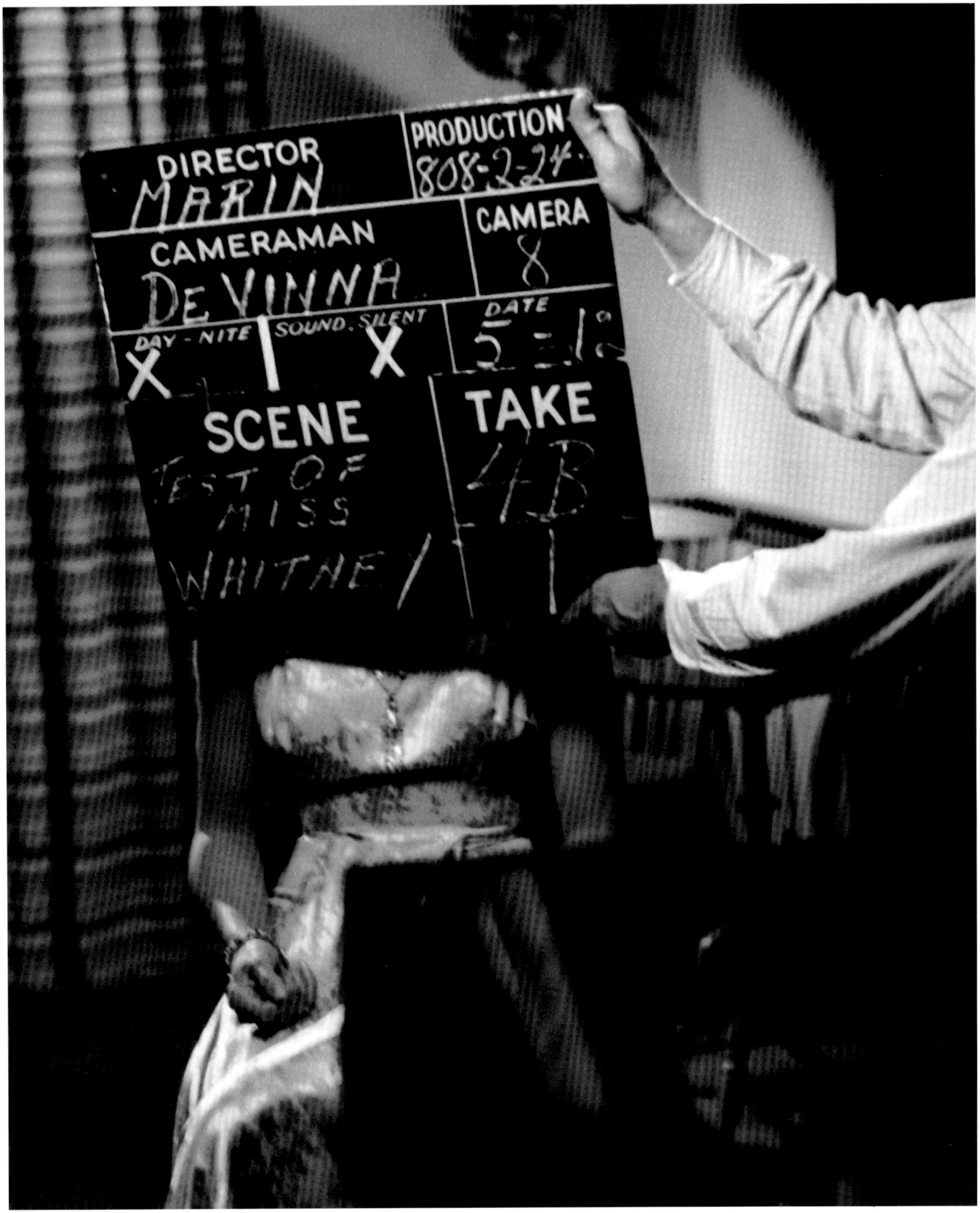
DIRECTOR
MARIN
PRODUCTION
808-2-24
CAMERAMAN
DE VINNA
CAMERA
8
DAY - NITE
SOUND. SILENT
DATE
SCENE
TEST OF
MISS
WHITNEY
TAKE
4B

Rosalie set, MGM back lot, 1938

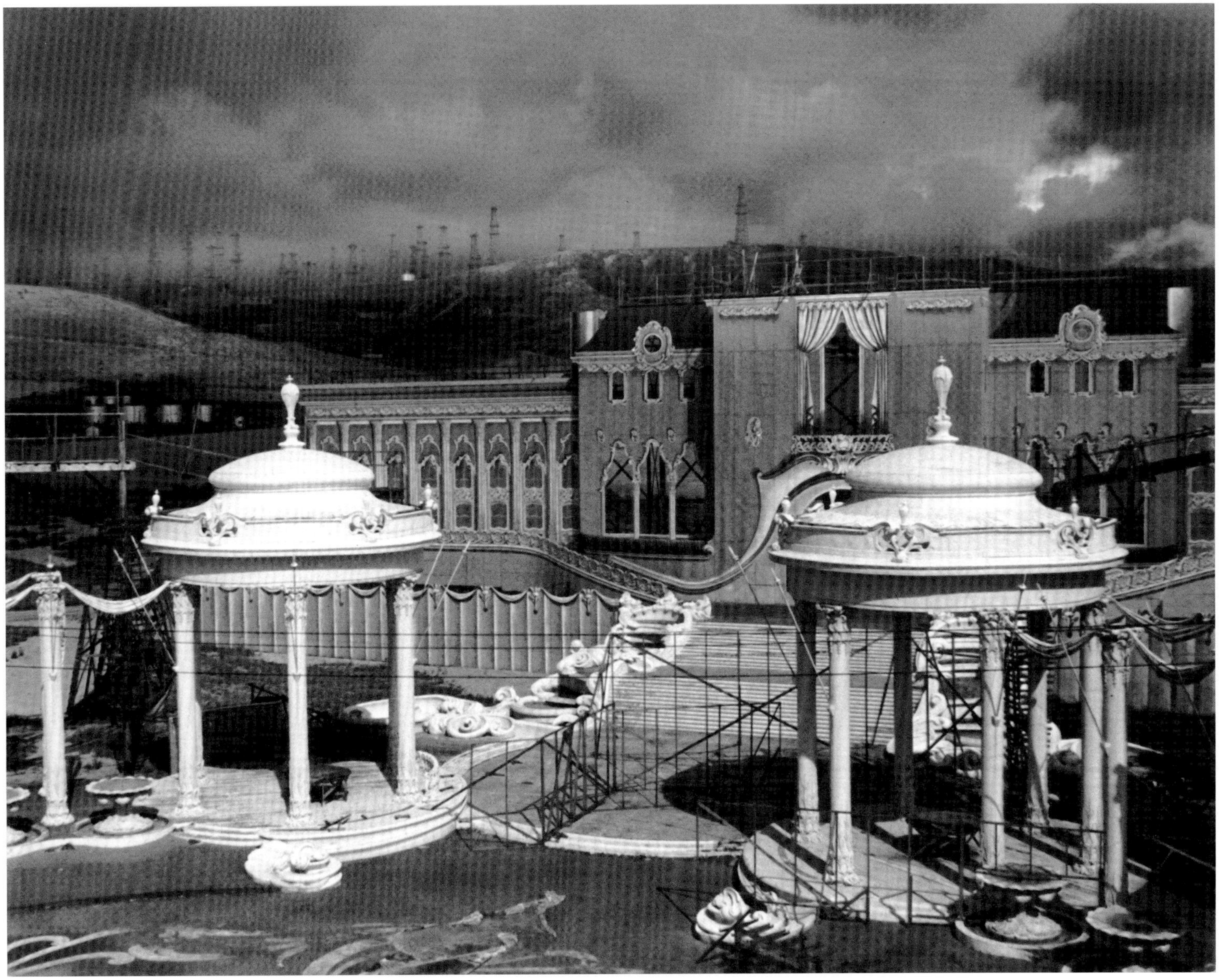

Victorian costume for *Marie Antoinette,* 1938

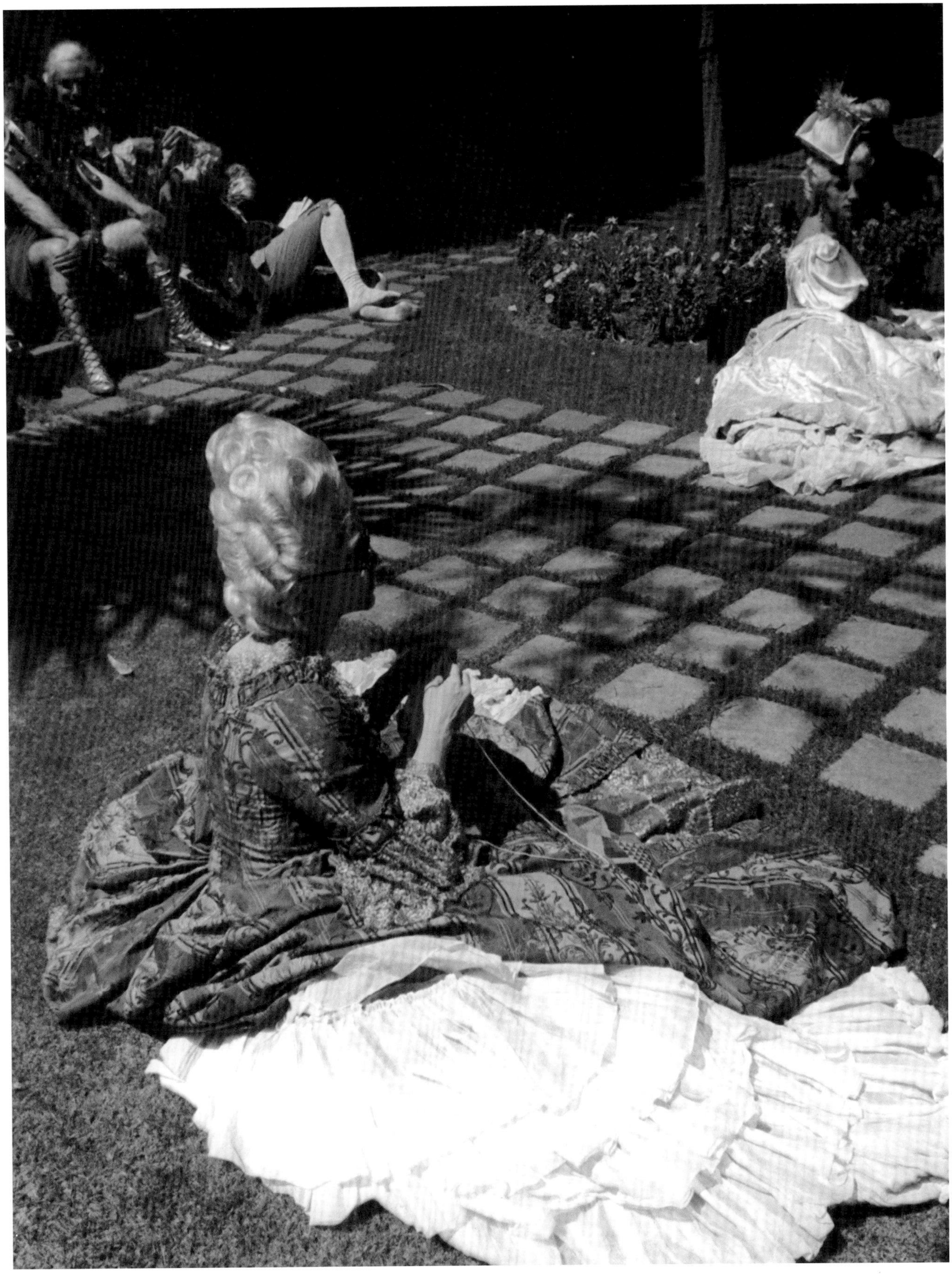

Sleeping extra, 1938

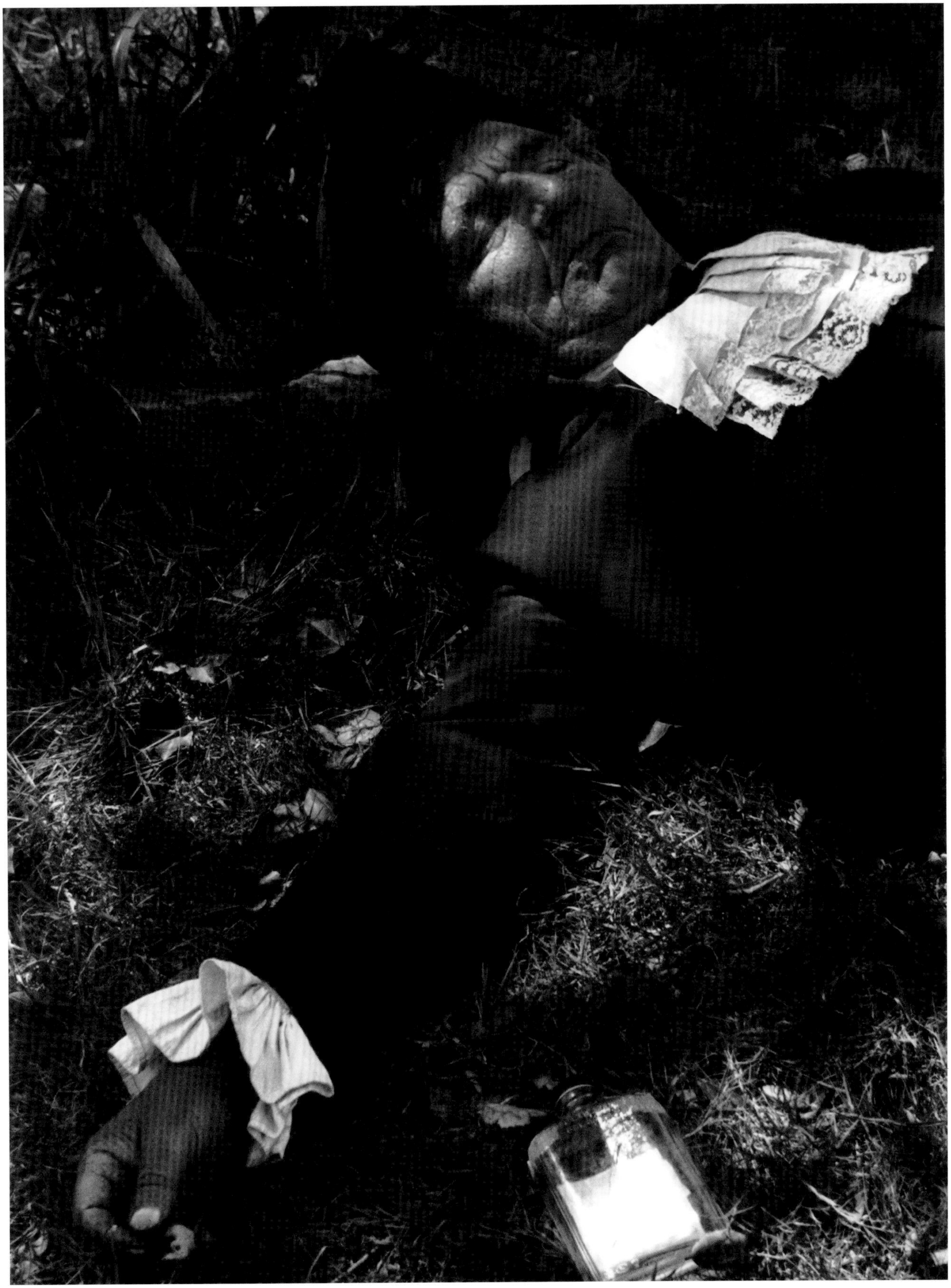

Josh Logan playing dead, 1938

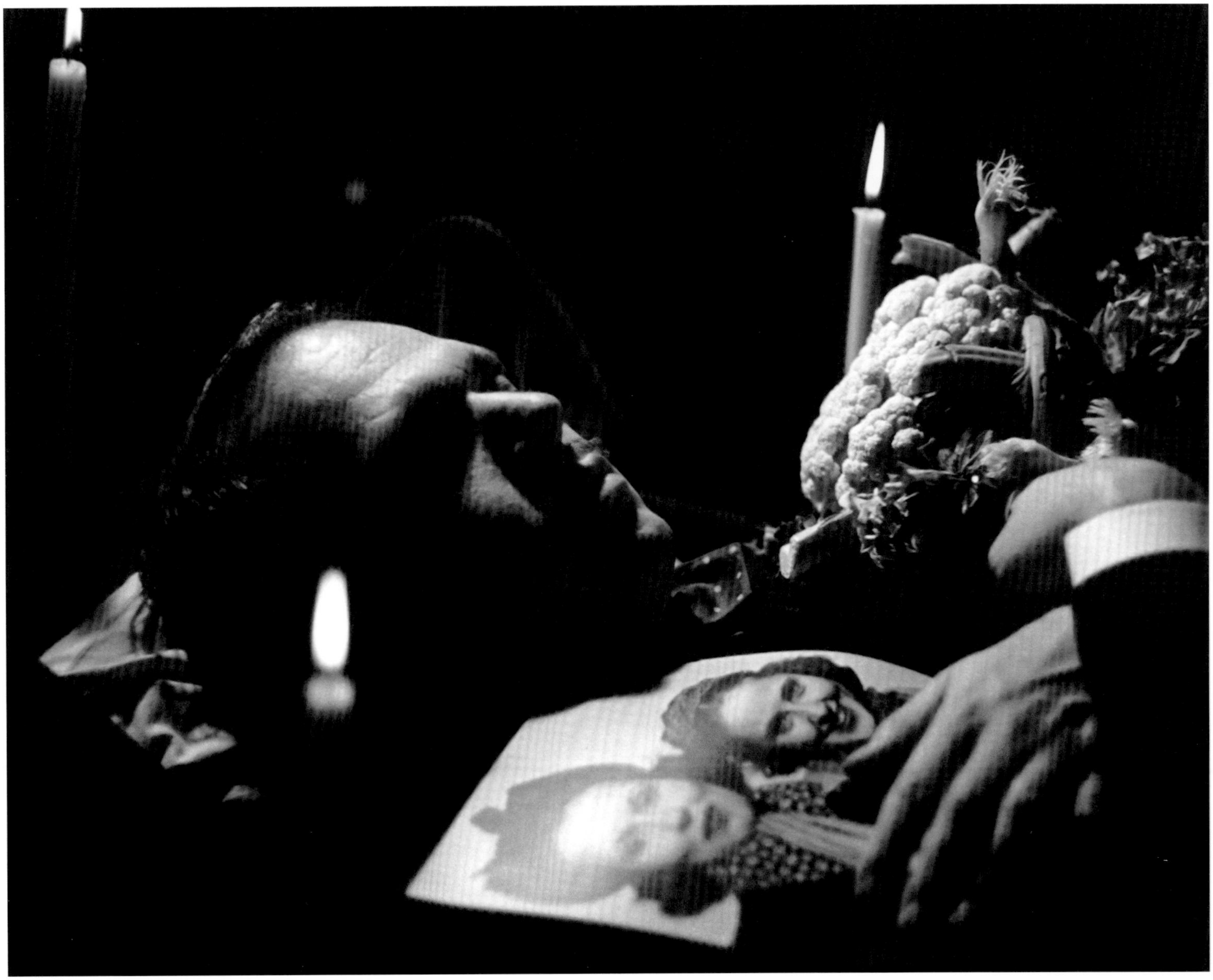

The card game, 1938

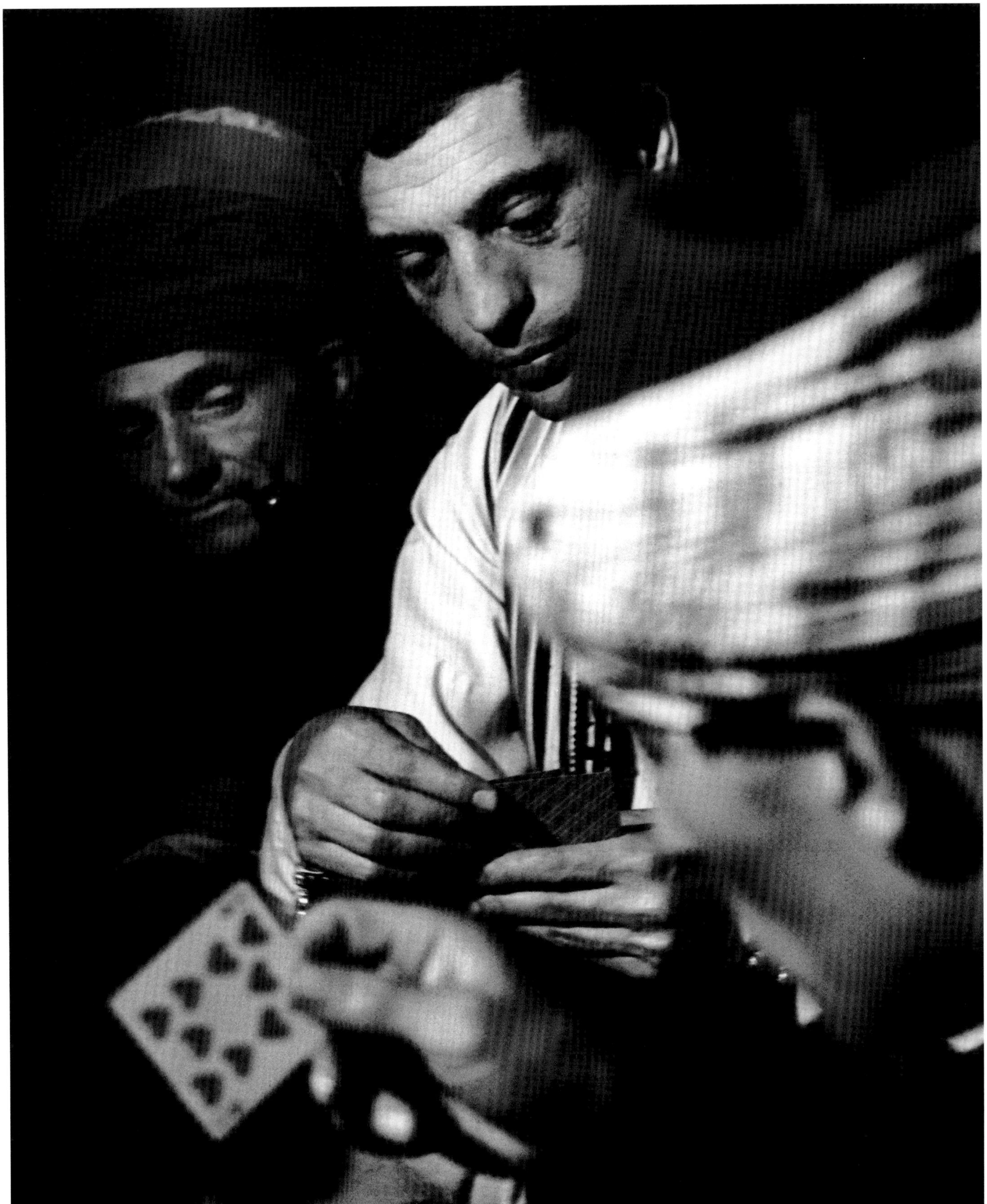

Chinese extras registering for studio work, 1938

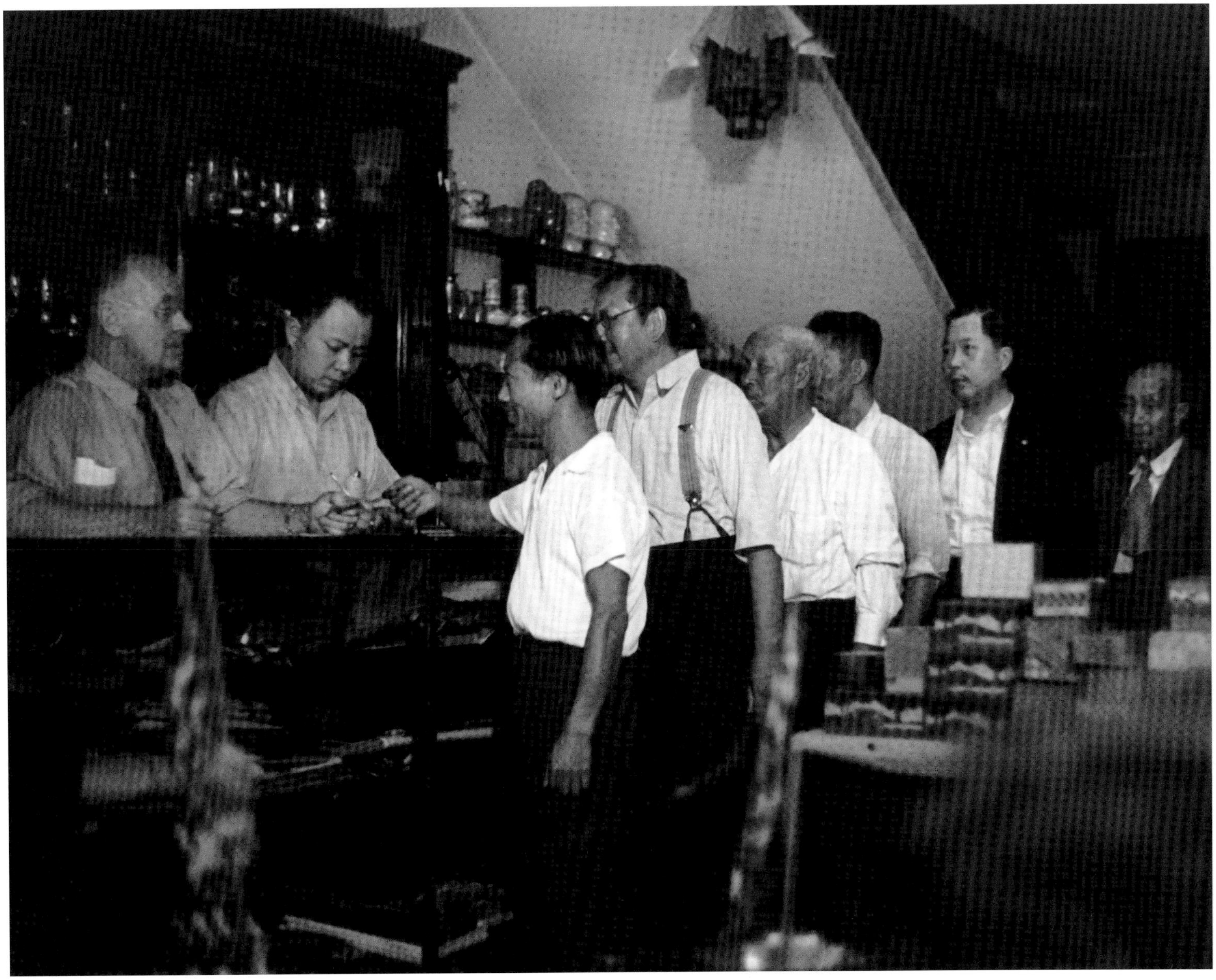

Clarence Muse reading newspaper, 1938

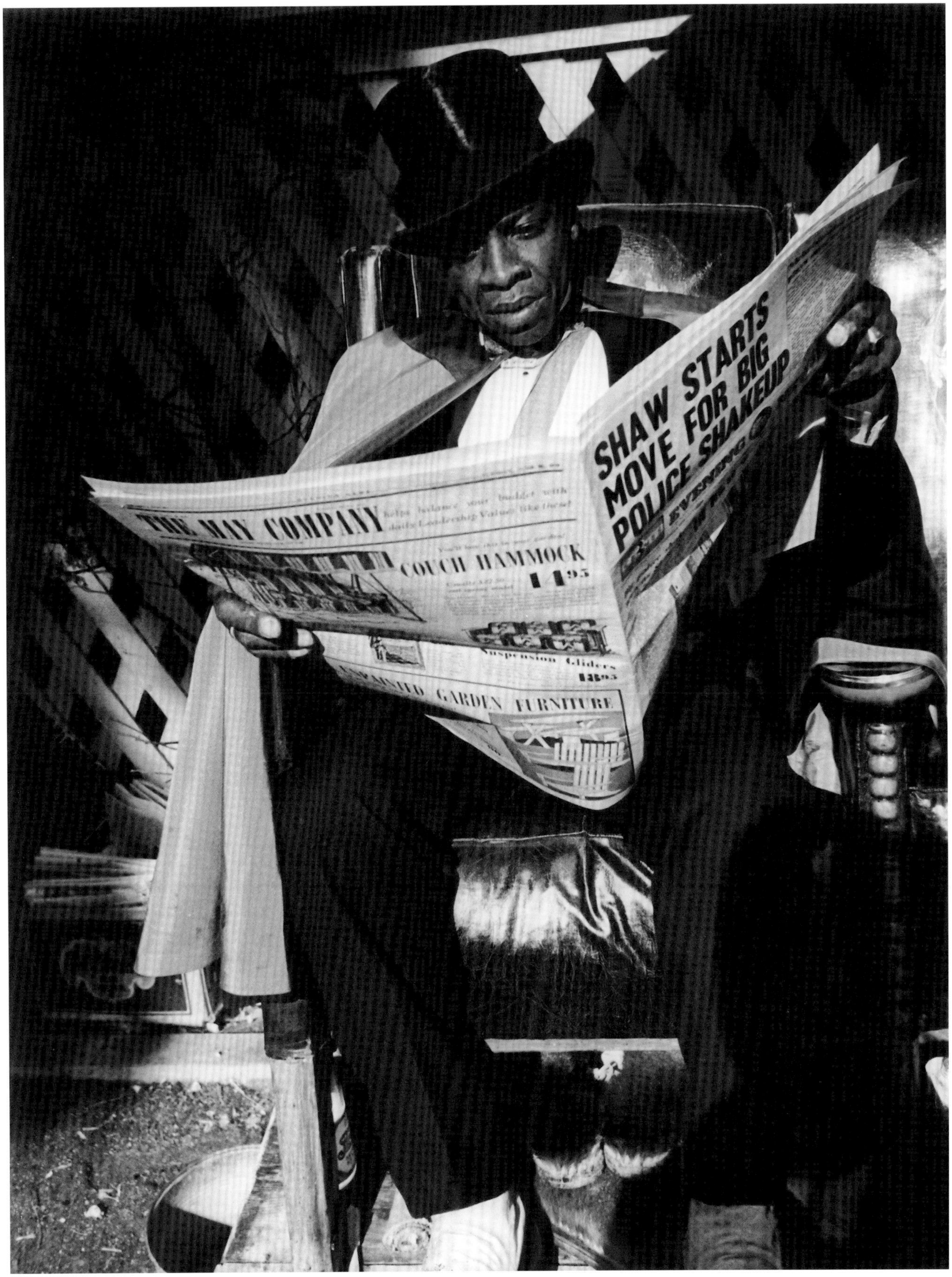
SHAW STARTS MOVE FOR BIG POLICE SHAKEUP
THE MAY COMPANY
COUCH HAMMOCK
Suspension Gliders
GARDEN FURNITURE

Laughing girl, Hollywood party, 1938

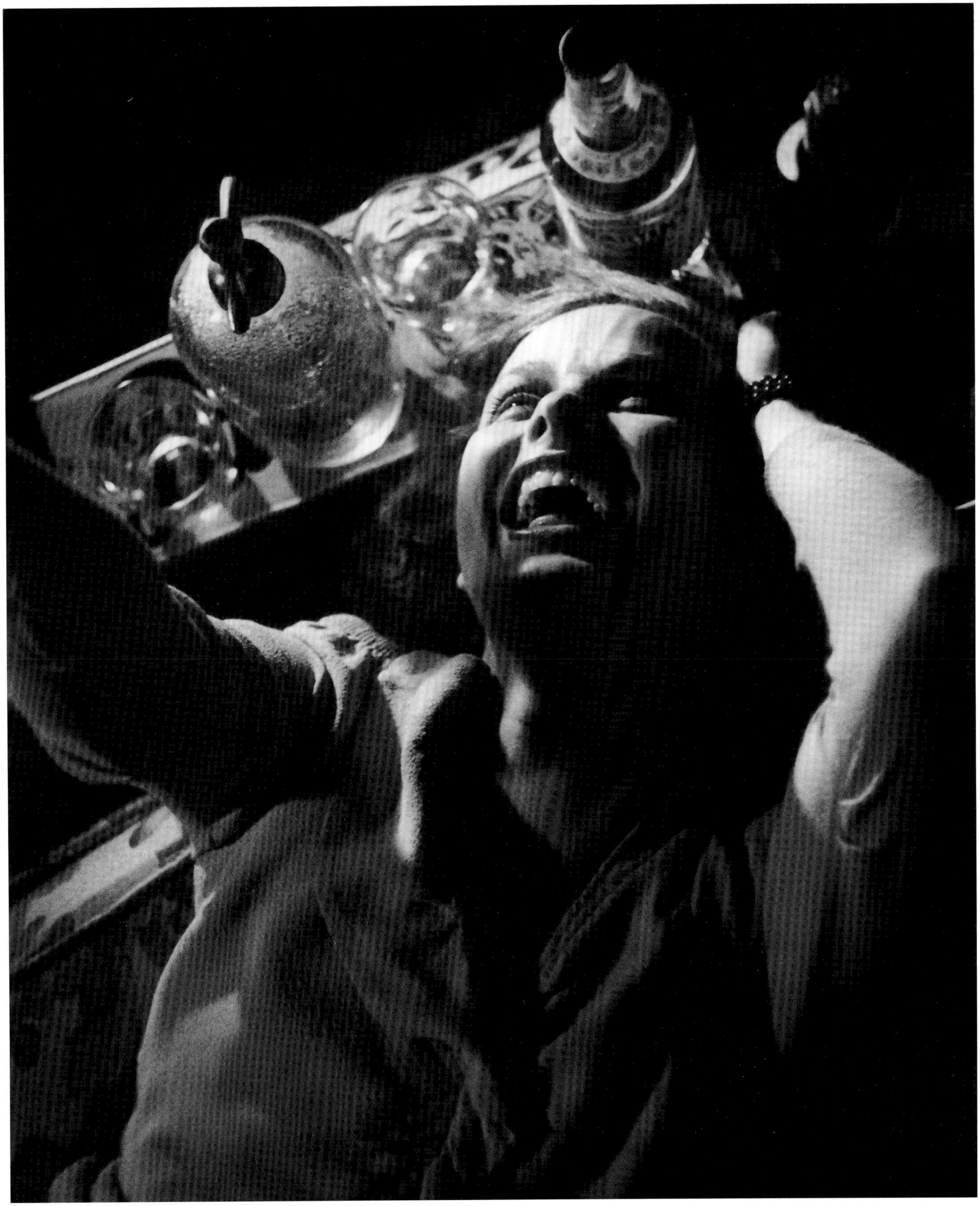

Ann Rutherford with dog posing for cameraman, 1938

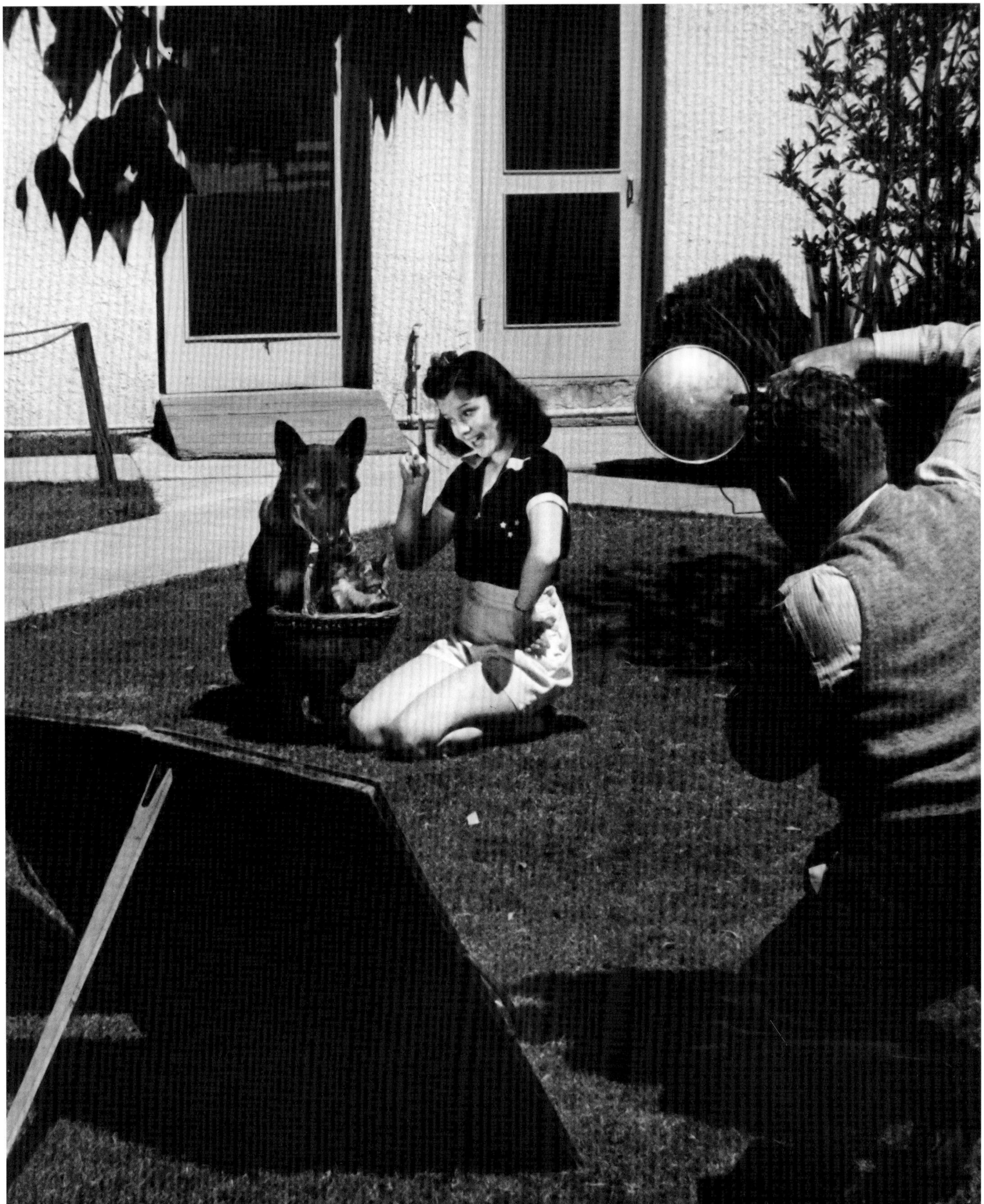

Reginald Gardner, Jeanette MacDonald, and Nelson Eddy, 1938

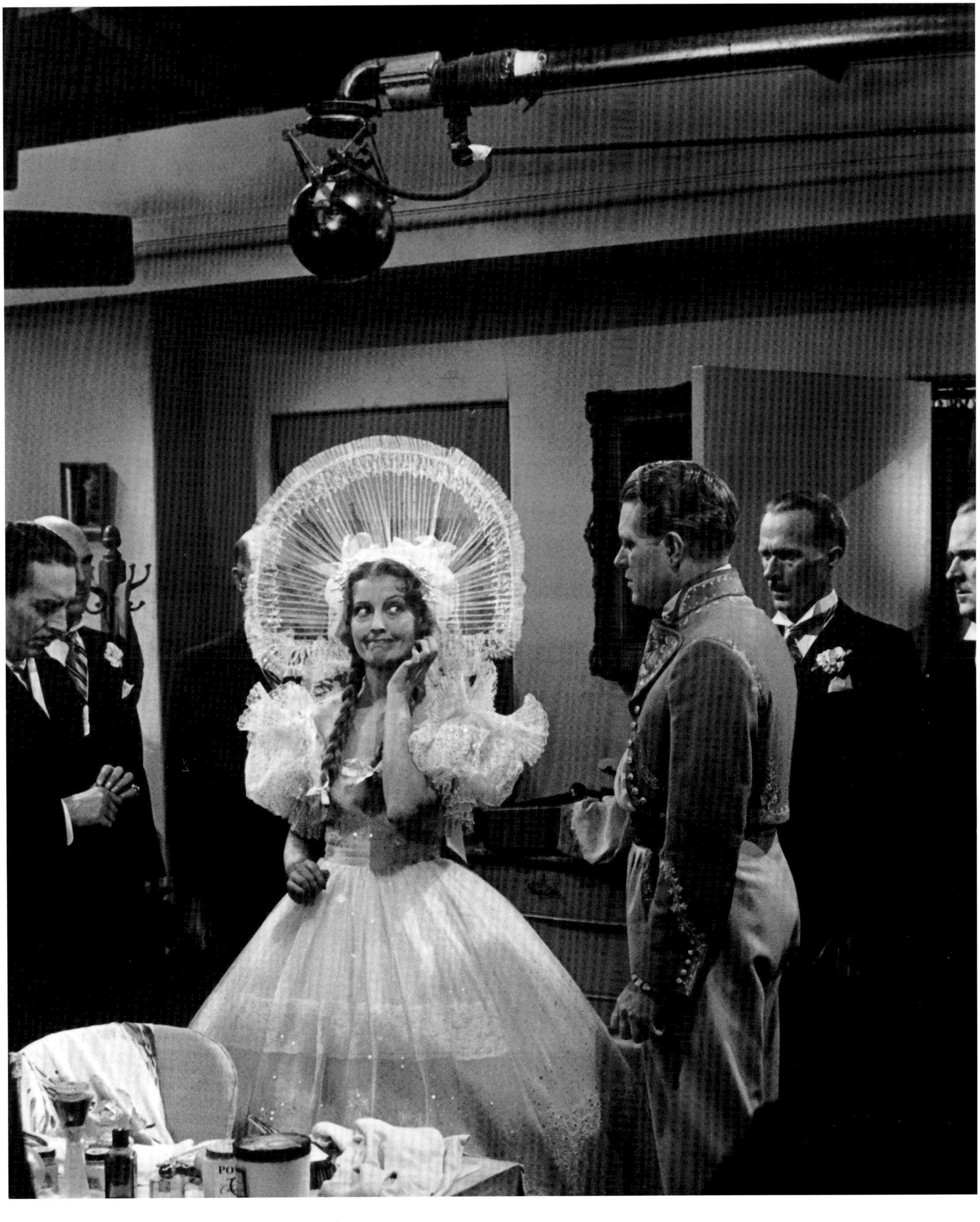

Fun in Movieland, 1938

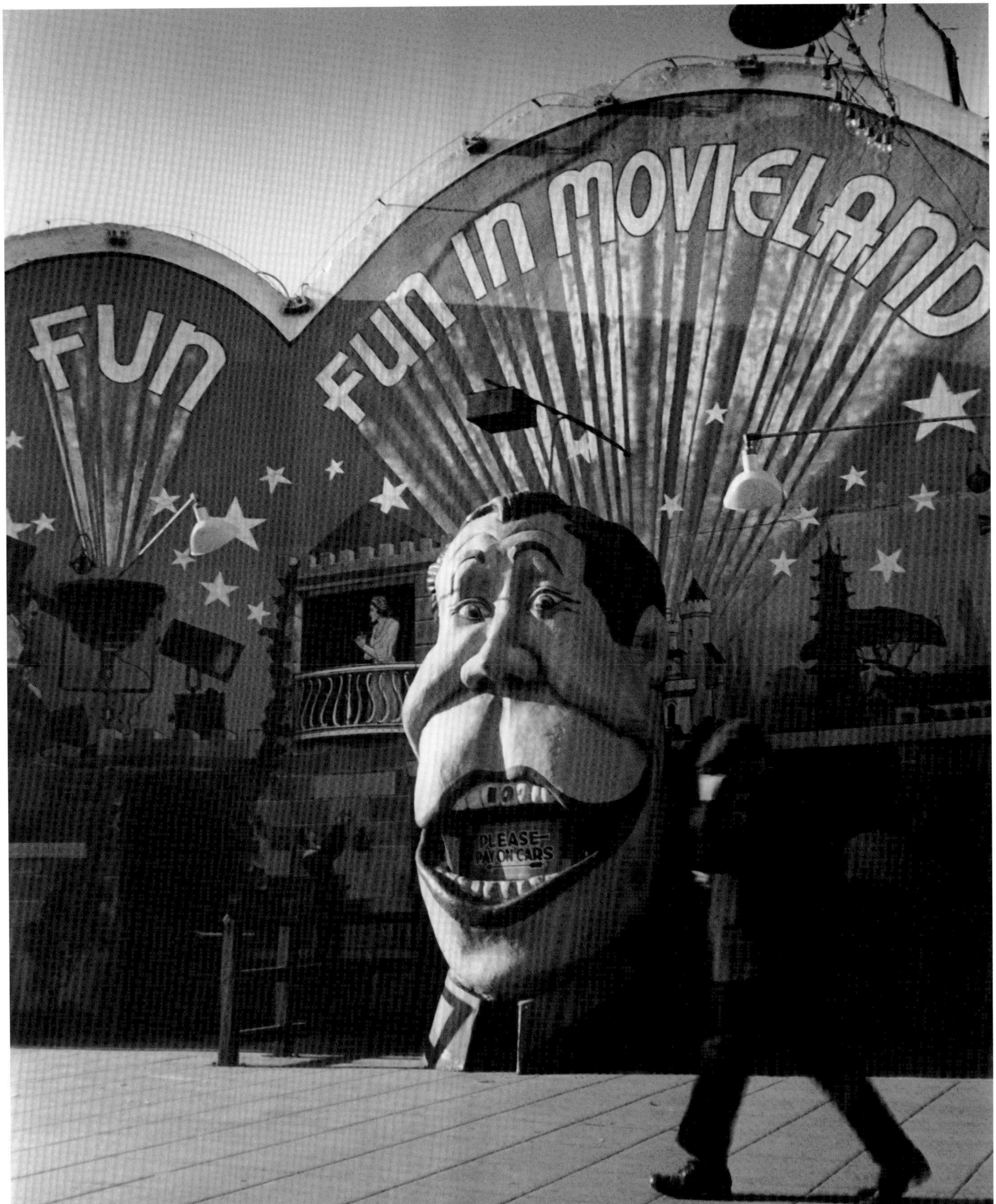
FUN
FUN IN MOVIELAND
PLEASE—
PAY ON CARS

Main Street, Los Angeles: "4 Hit Pictures 10 Cents," 1938

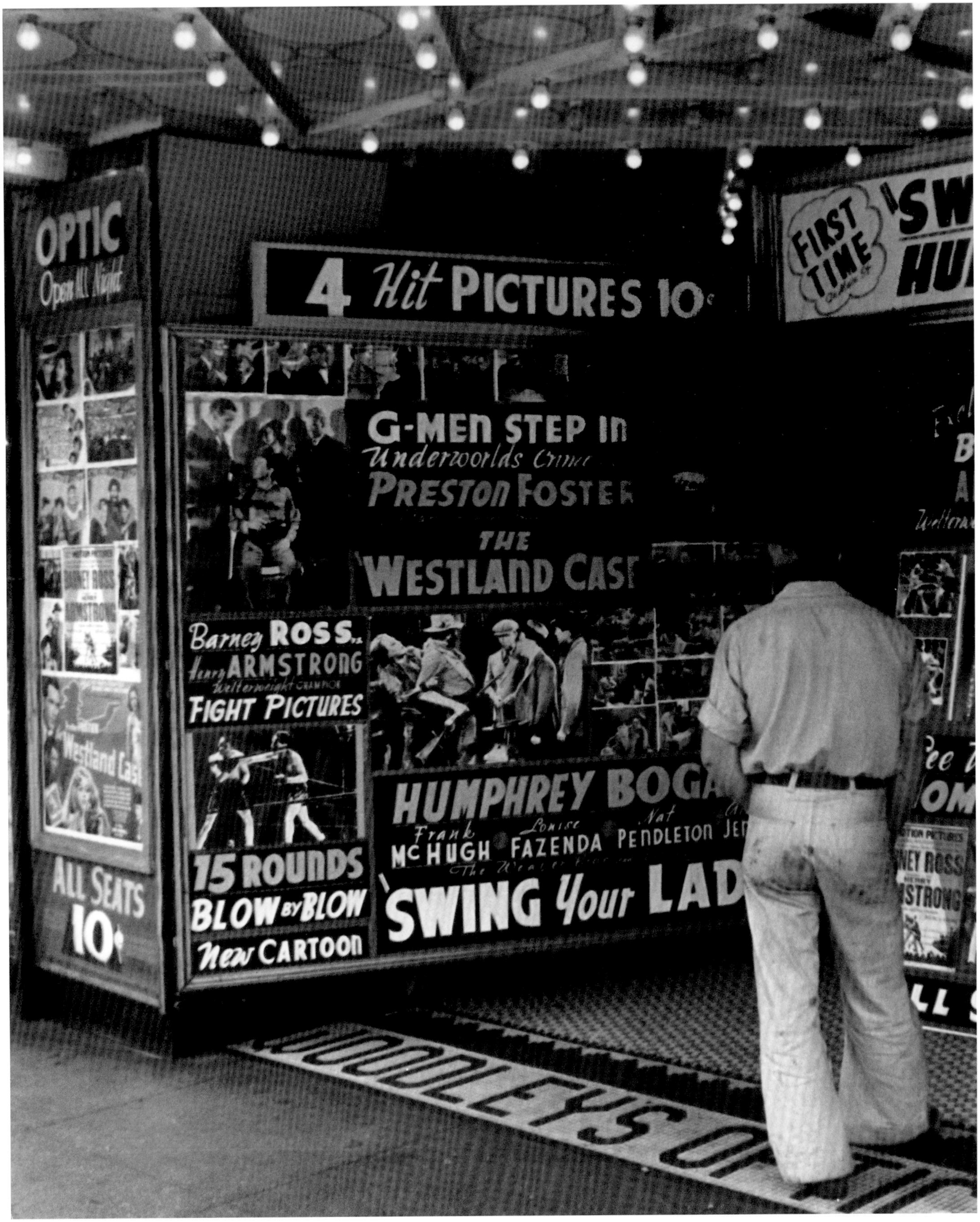
OPTIC
Open All Night
4 Hit PICTURES 10¢
FIRST TIME
G-MEN STEP IN
Underworlds
PRESTON FOSTER
THE
Barney ROSS
Henry ARMSTRONG
Welterweight CHAMPION
FIGHT PICTURES
15 ROUNDS
BLOW BY BLOW
New CARTOON
Frank McHUGH
Louise FAZENDA
Nat PENDLETON
ALL SEATS 10¢

Guides to the Stars, Sunset Boulevard, 1938

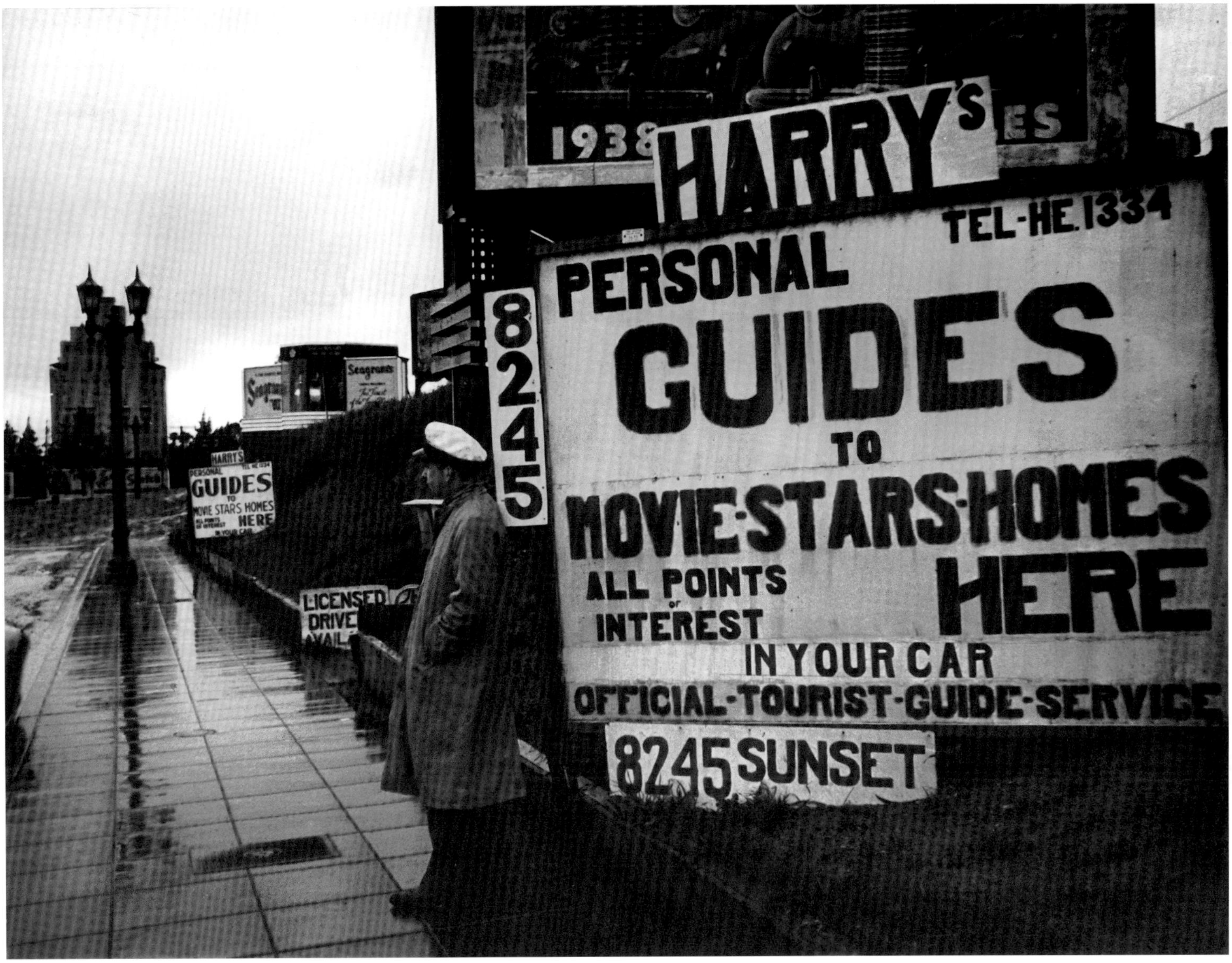
1938
HARRY'S
TEL-HE.1334
PERSONAL
GUIDES
TO
MOVIE-STARS-HOMES
ALL POINTS OF INTEREST
HERE
IN YOUR CAR
OFFICIAL-TOURIST-GUIDE-SERVICE
8245
8245 SUNSET
LICENSED
DRIVE

California State Employment Service, 1938

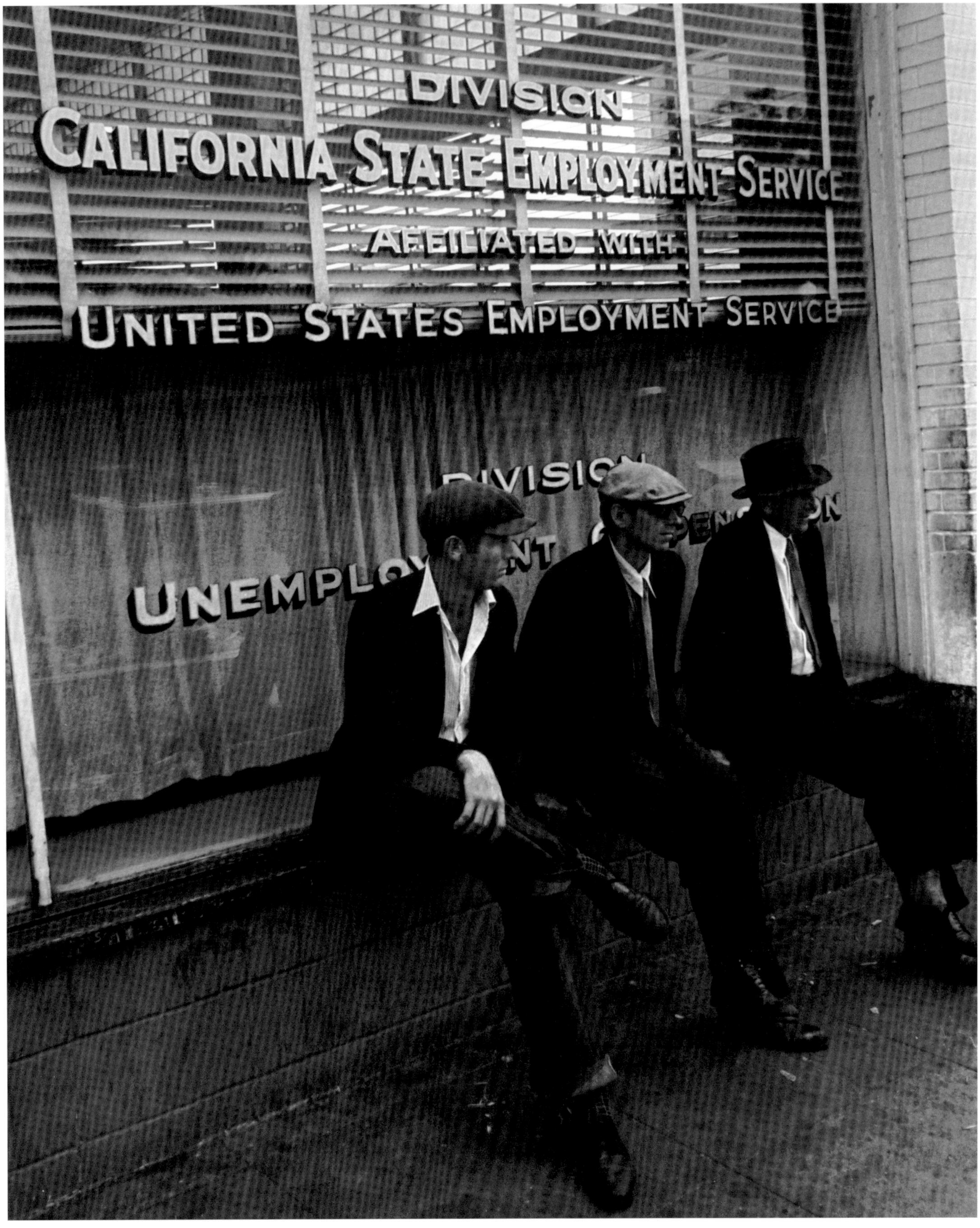
DIVISION
CALIFORNIA STATE EMPLOYMENT SERVICE
AFFILIATED WITH
UNITED STATES EMPLOYMENT SERVICE

Jimmy Stewart signing autographs for fans, 1938

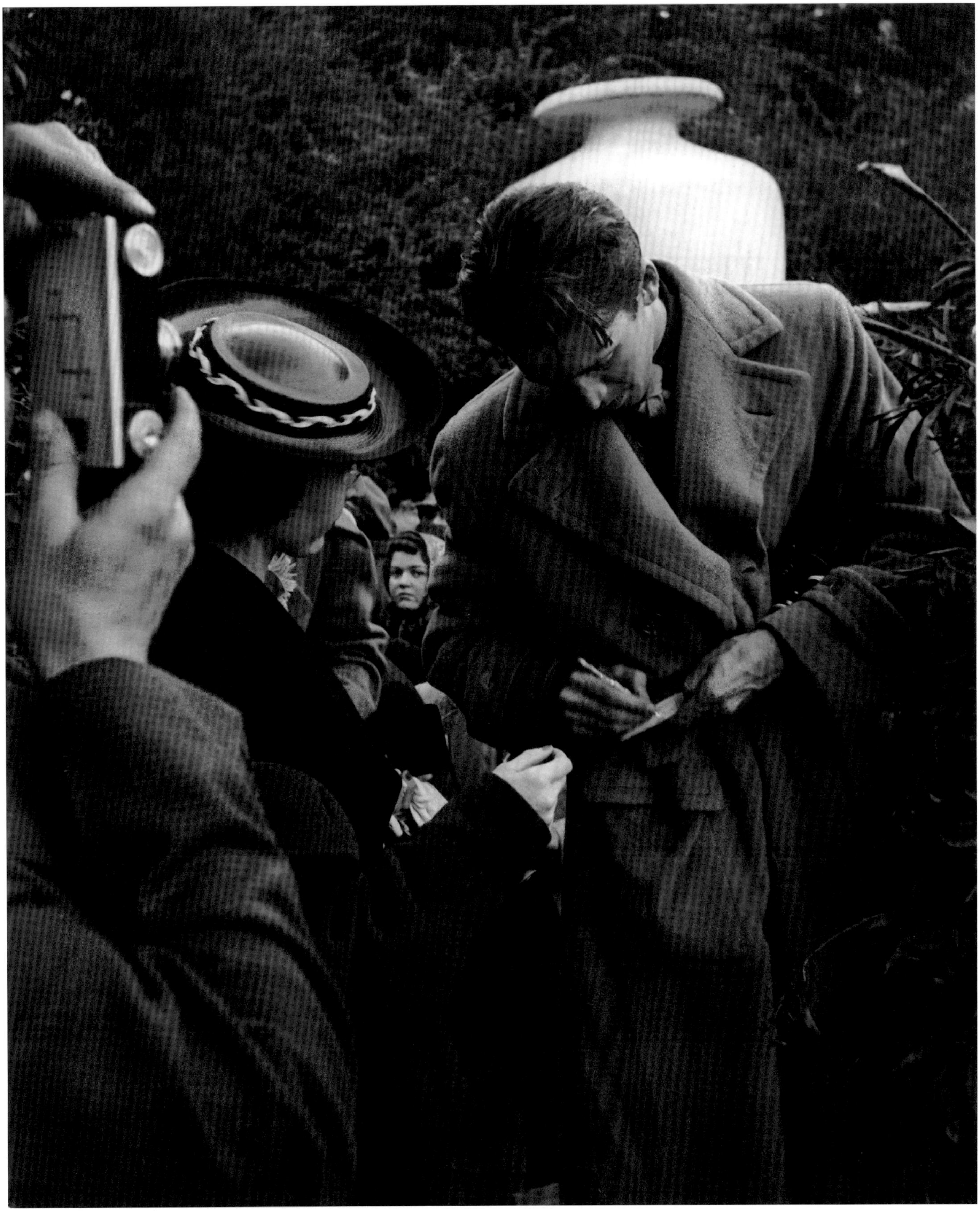

Burgess Meredith, 1938

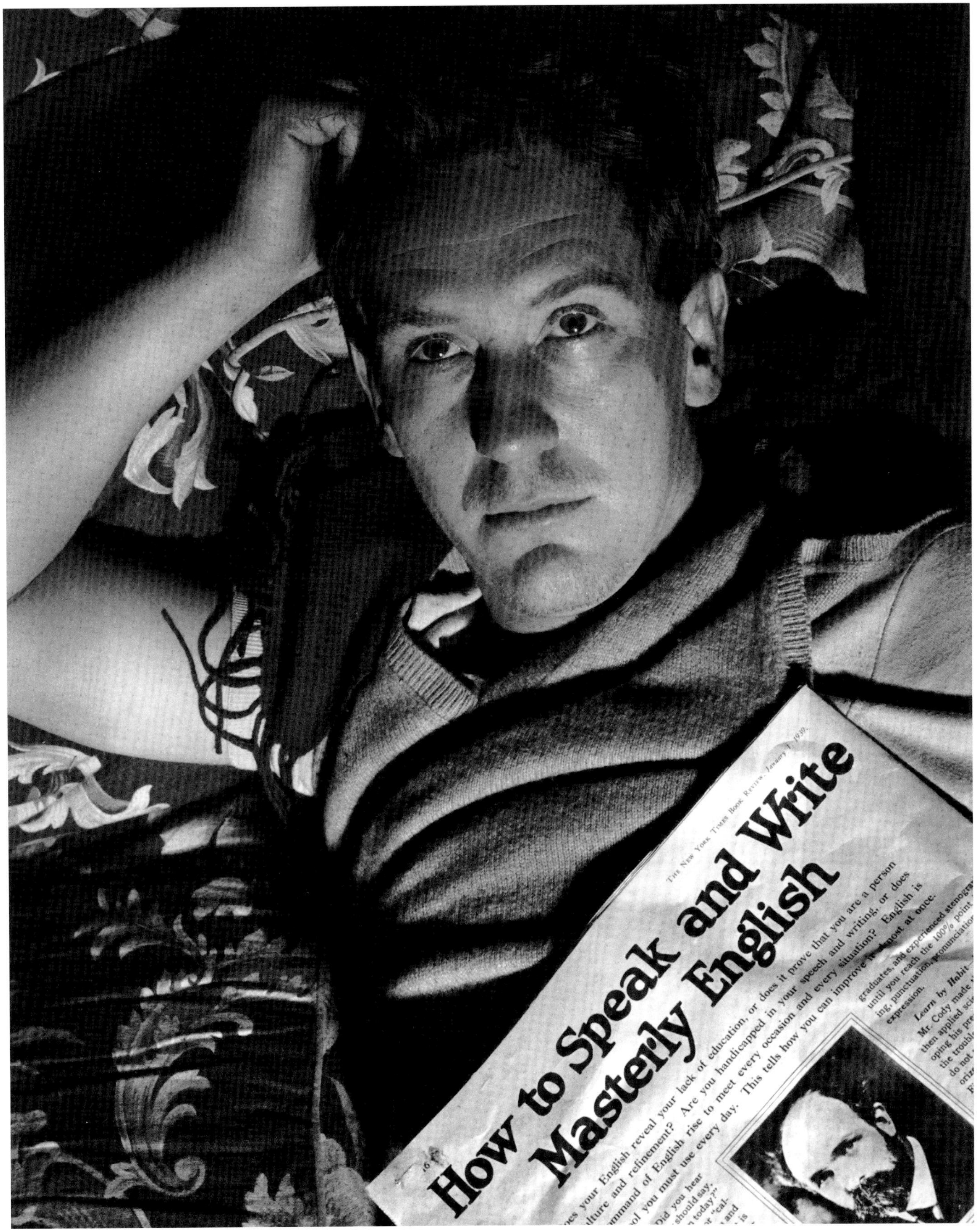
How to Speak and Write Masterly English

Smoking woman talking on phone, 1938

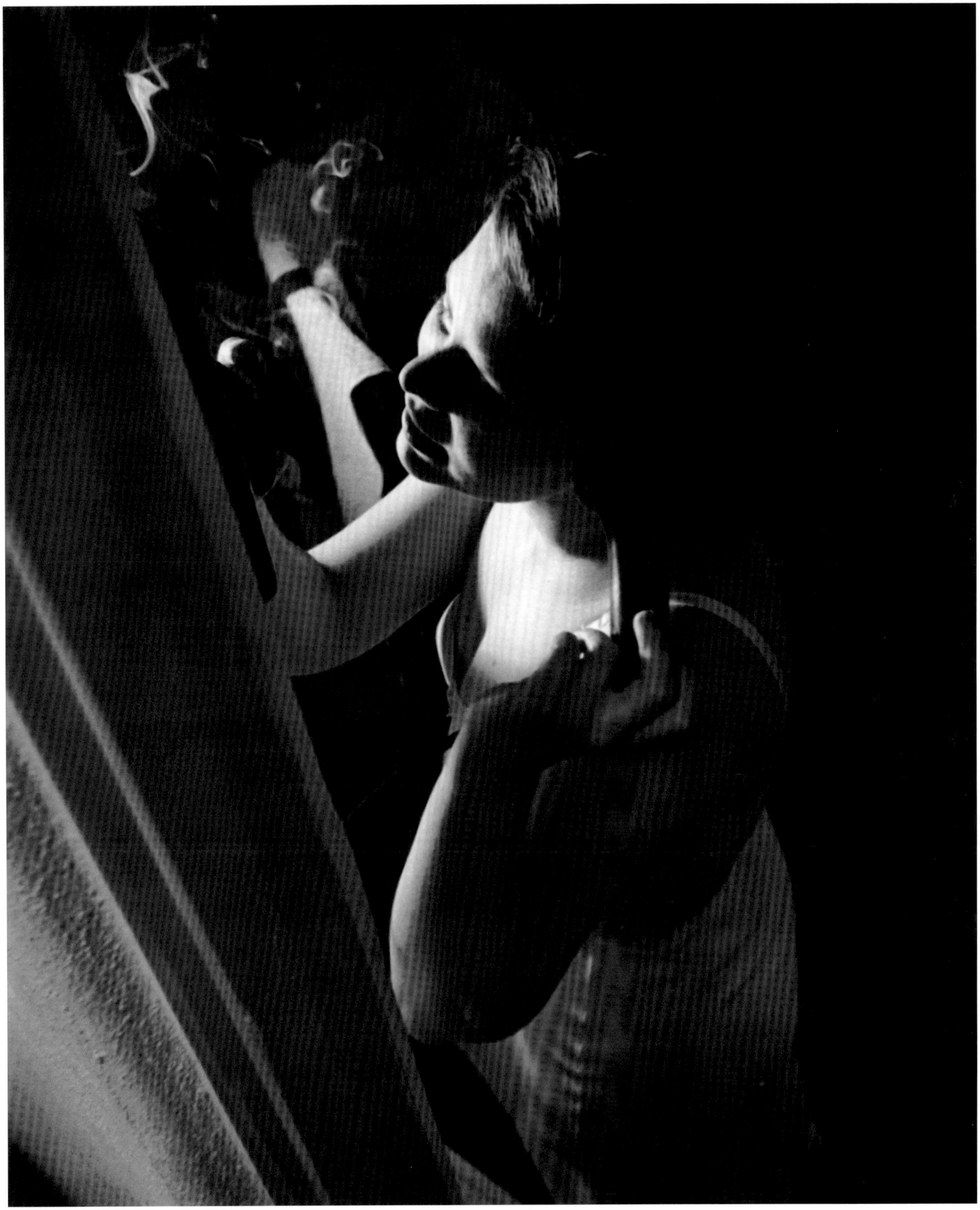

Jimmy Stewart and Olivia de Havilland lying in grass, 1938

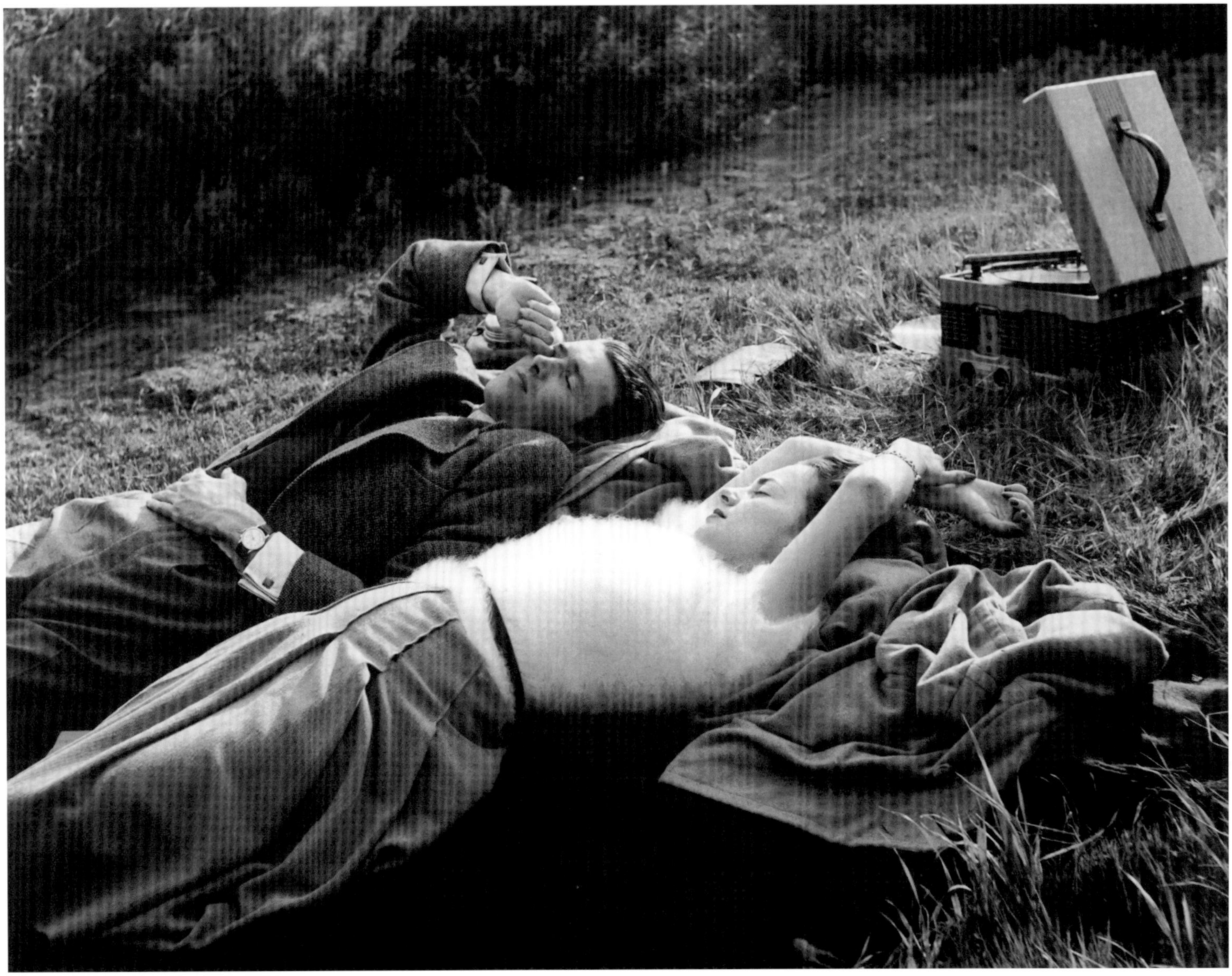

Norma Shearer and Jimmy Stewart in boat, 1938

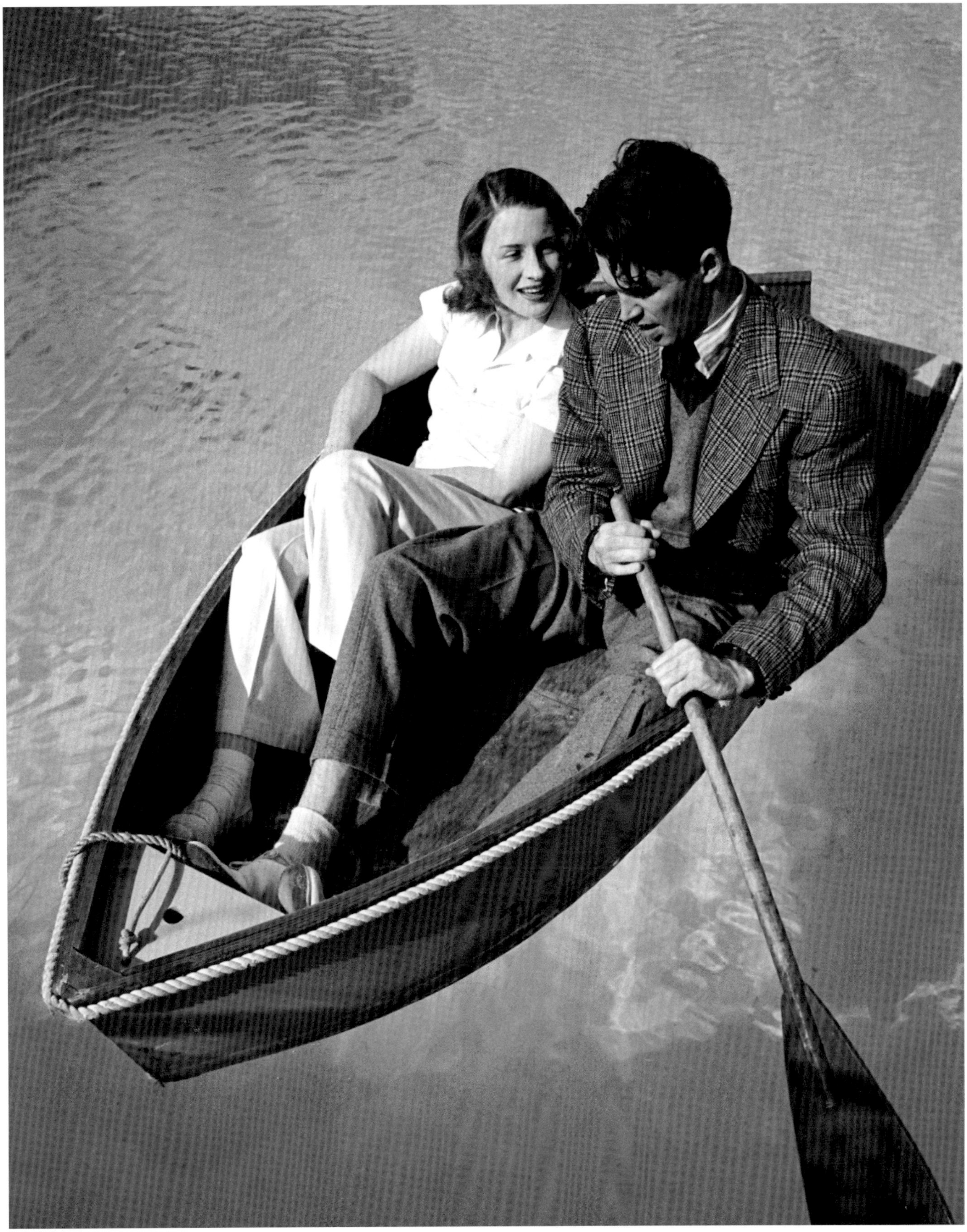

Shriners parade at night, 1937

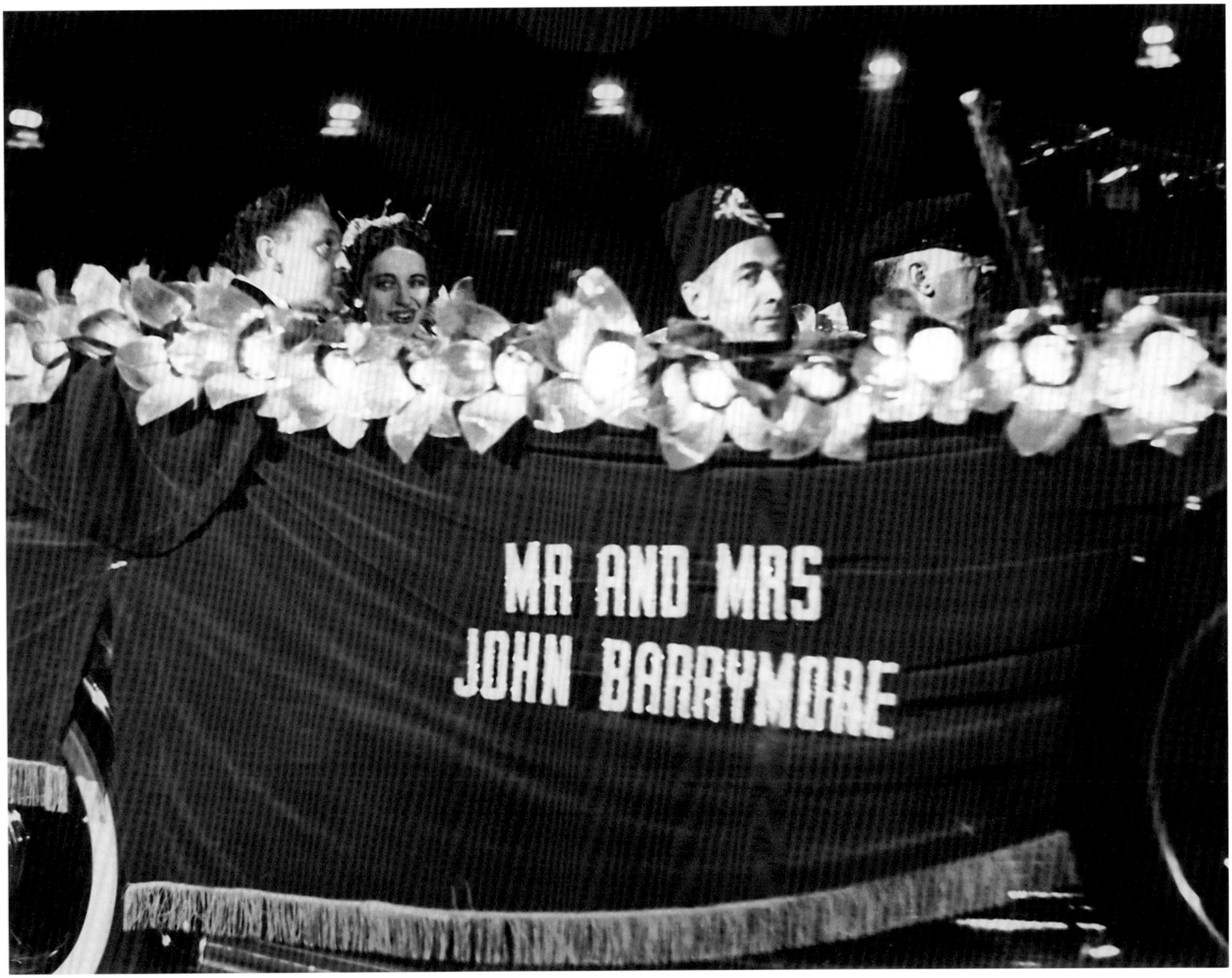
MR AND MRS
JOHN BARRYMORE

The Road to Glory, Main Street, Los Angeles, 1937

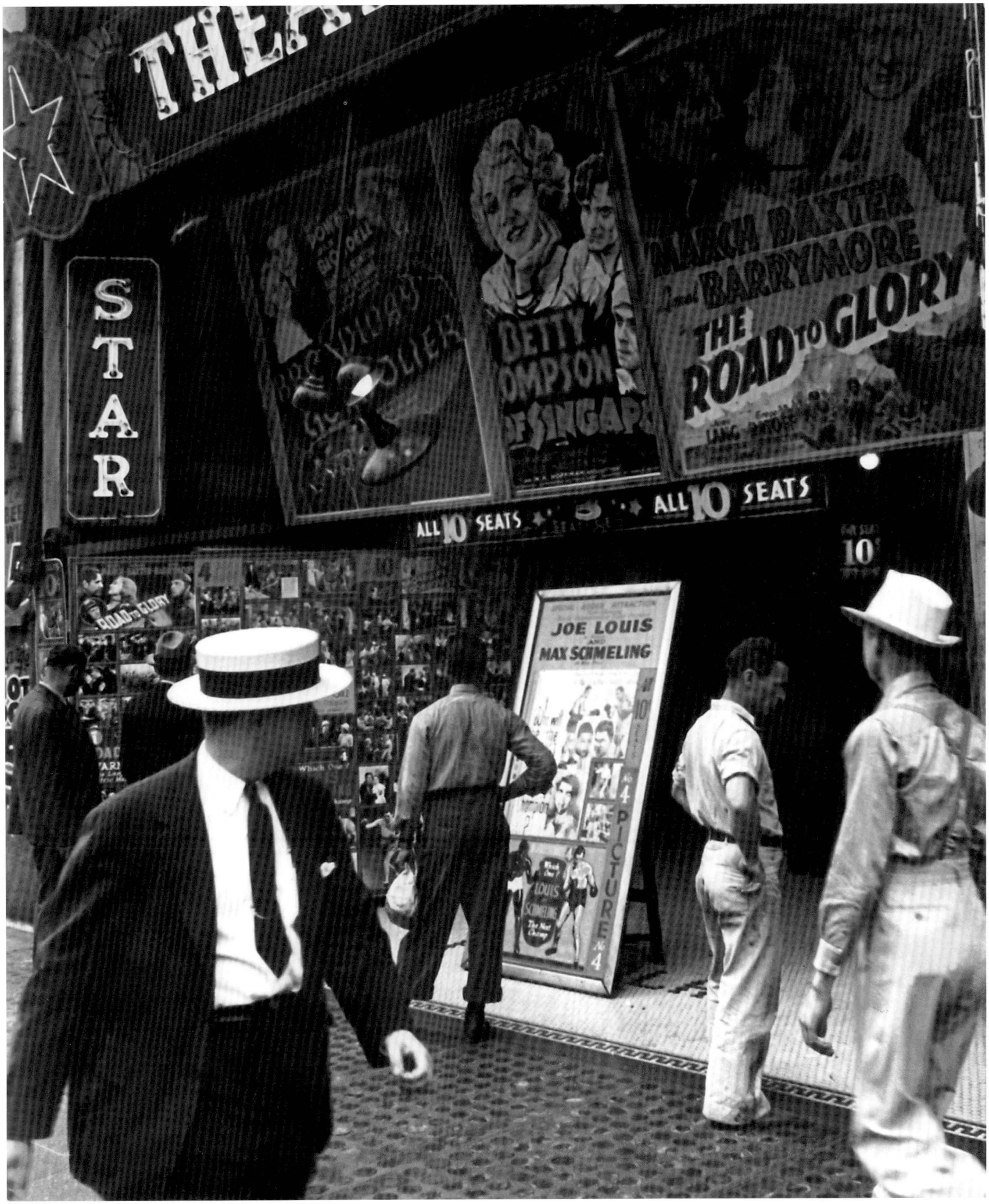
STAR
MARCH BAXTER
BARRYMORE
THE ROAD TO GLORY
ALL 10¢ SEATS
ALL 10¢ SEATS
JOE LOUIS
AND
MAX SCHMELING
PICTURE No 4

"Sex—5 cents," 1938

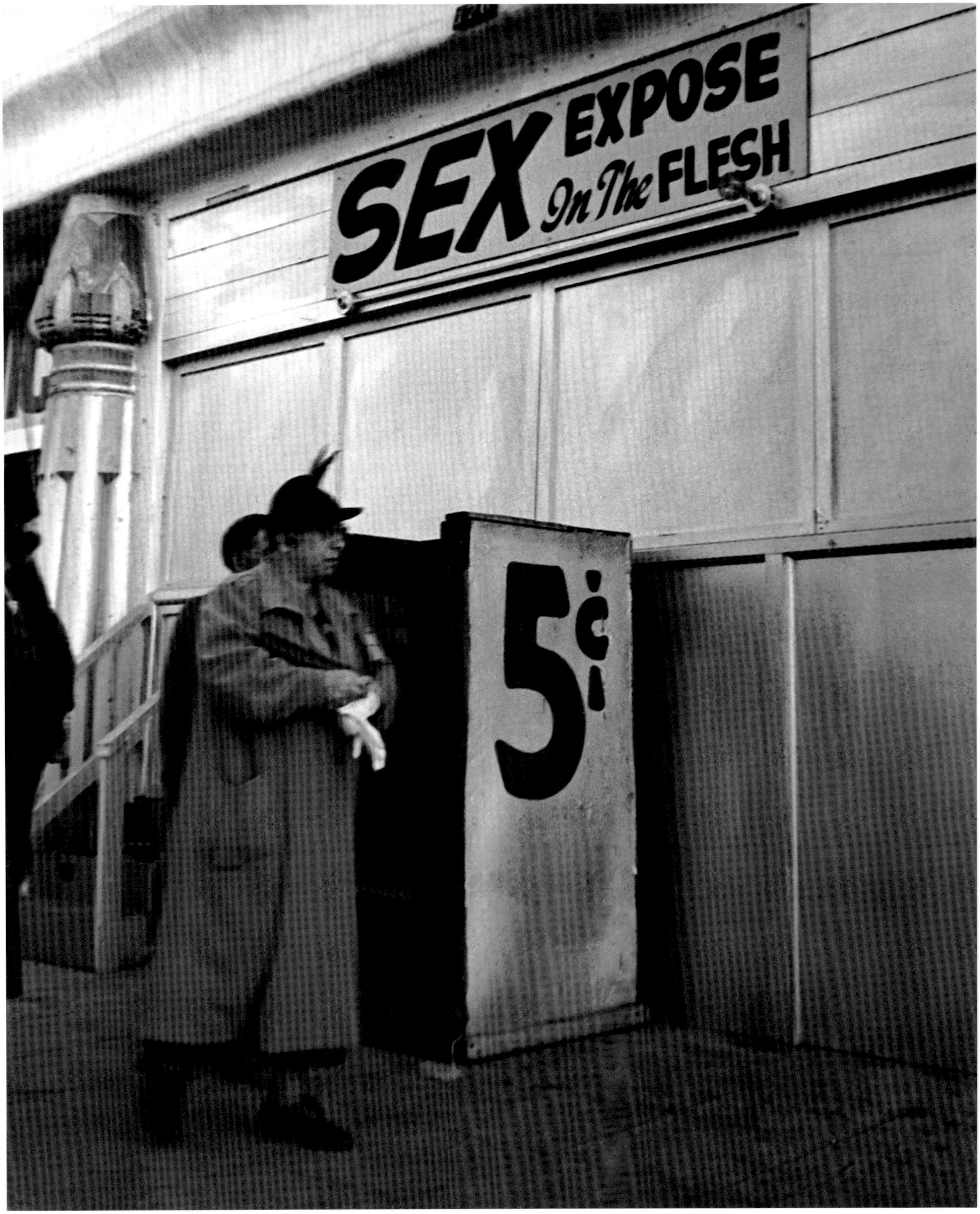
SEX
EXPOSE
In The FLESH
5¢

Steak house diner shaped like a frog, 1938

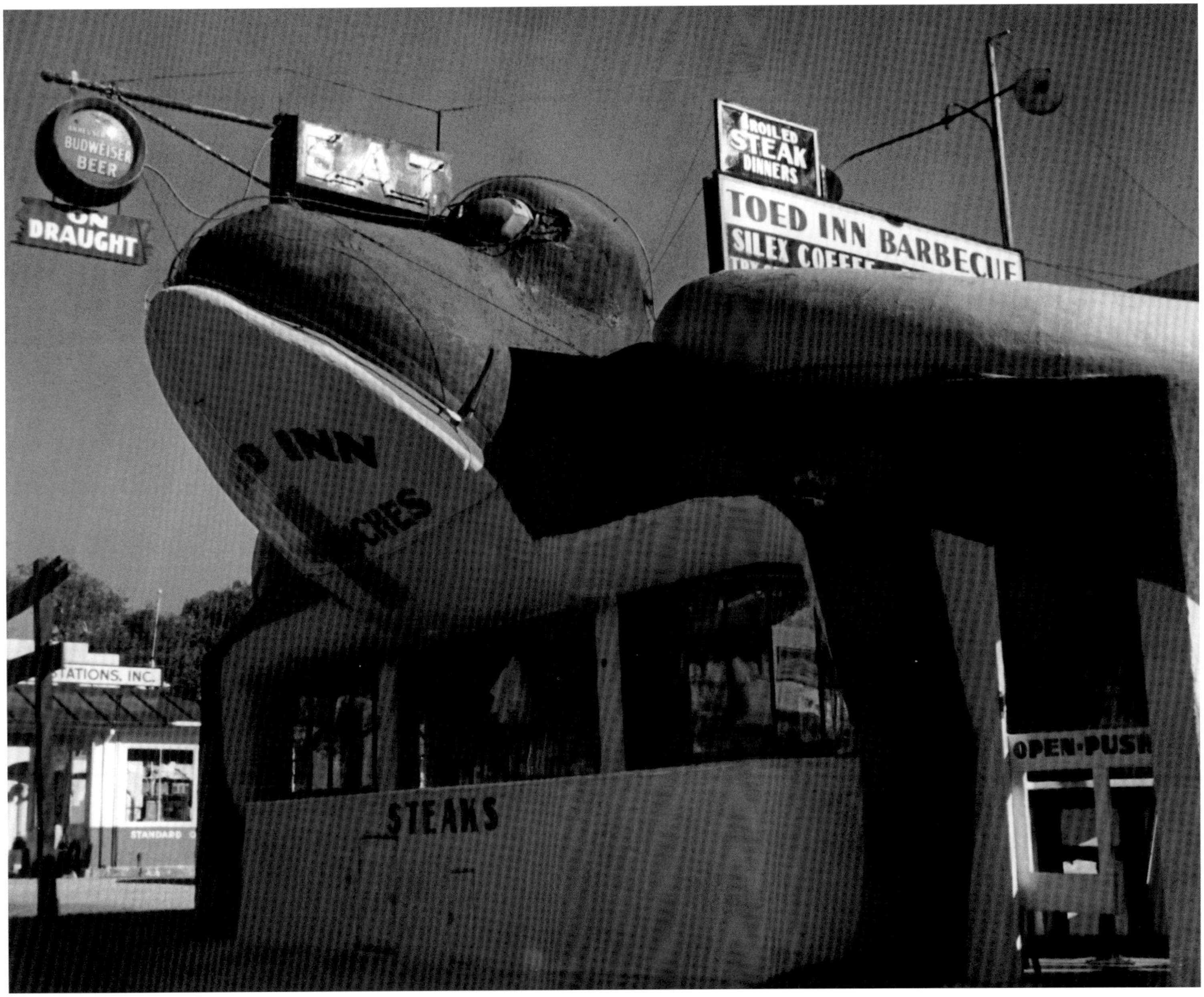
BUDWEISER BEER
ON DRAUGHT
STEAK
DINNERS
TOED INN BARBECUE
STATIONS, INC.
STEAKS

Serving food at the drive-in, 1938

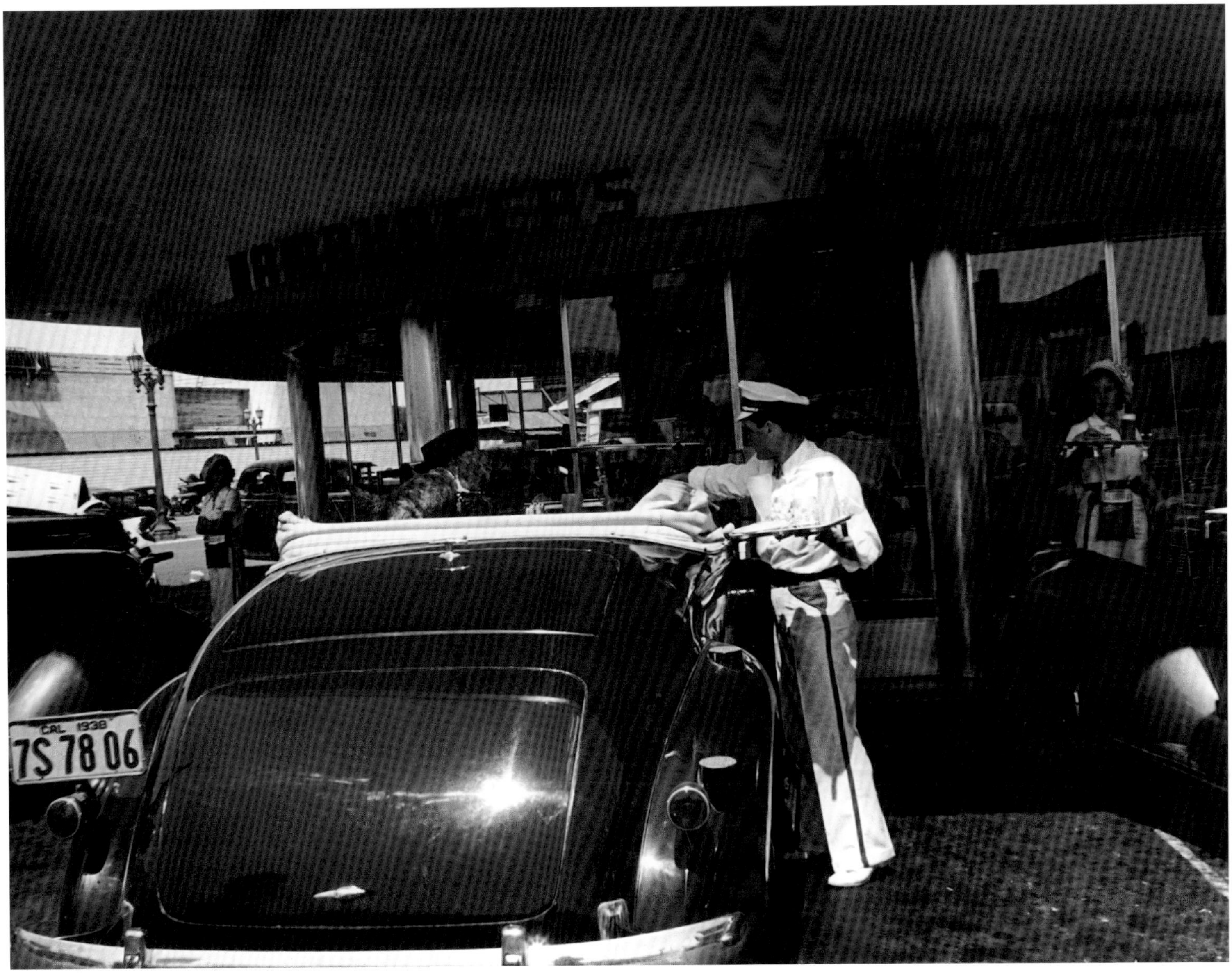
CAL 1938
7S 78 06

Drive-in eating stand, 1937

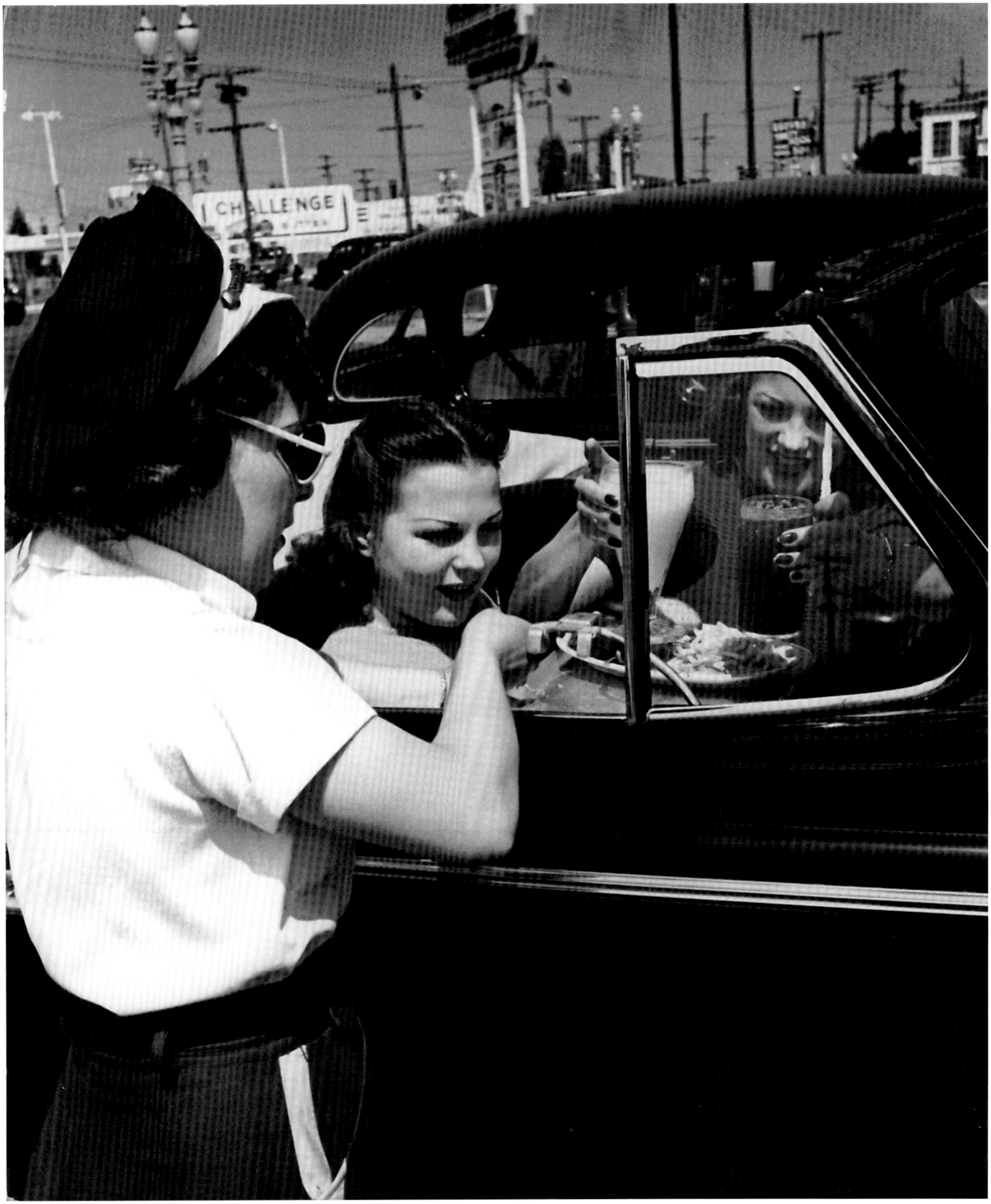
CHALLENGE

The Brown Derby, Wilshire Boulevard, 1938

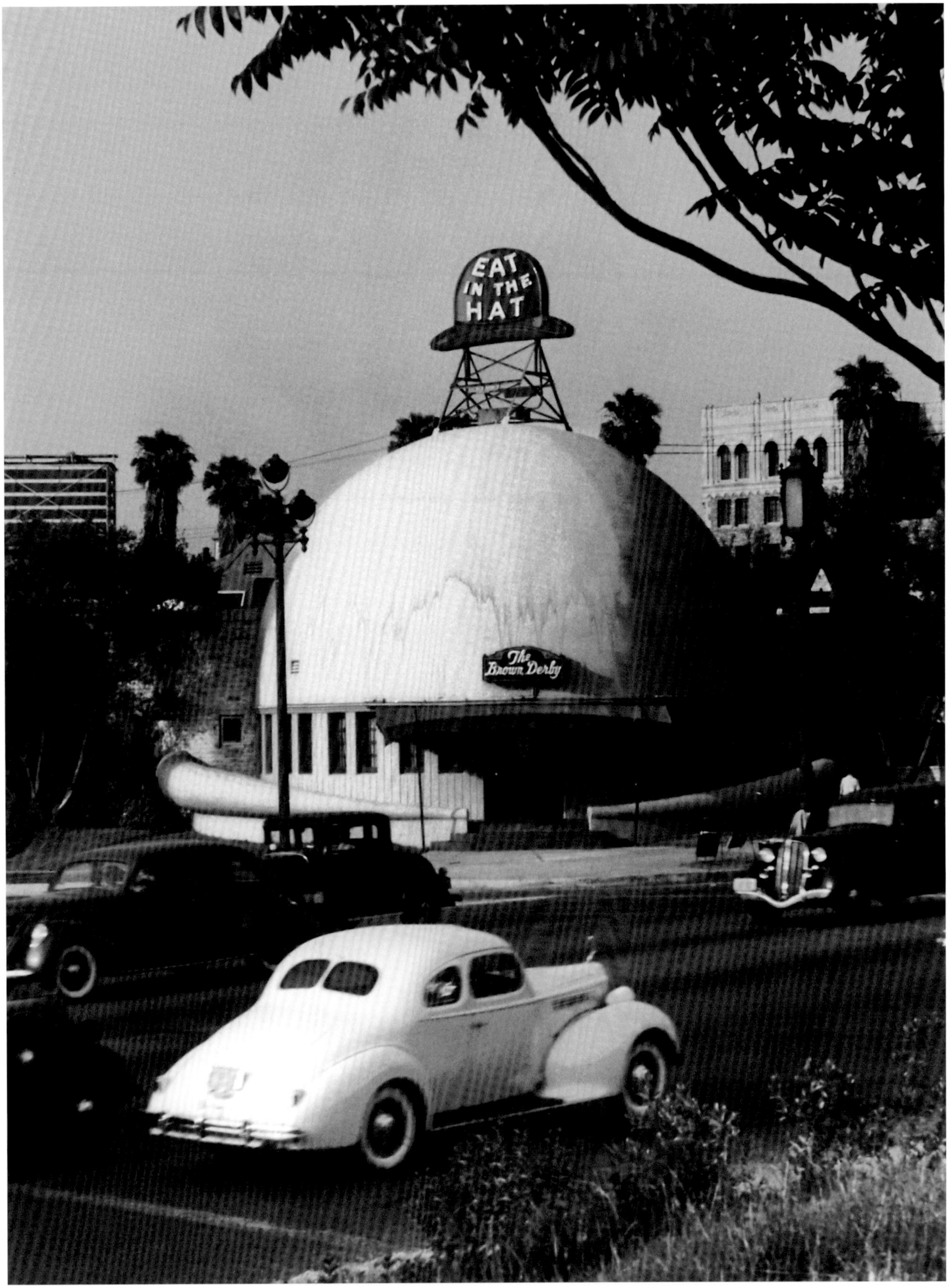
EAT
IN THE
HAT
The
Brown Derby

Windmill, street lamp, traffic signal, 1938

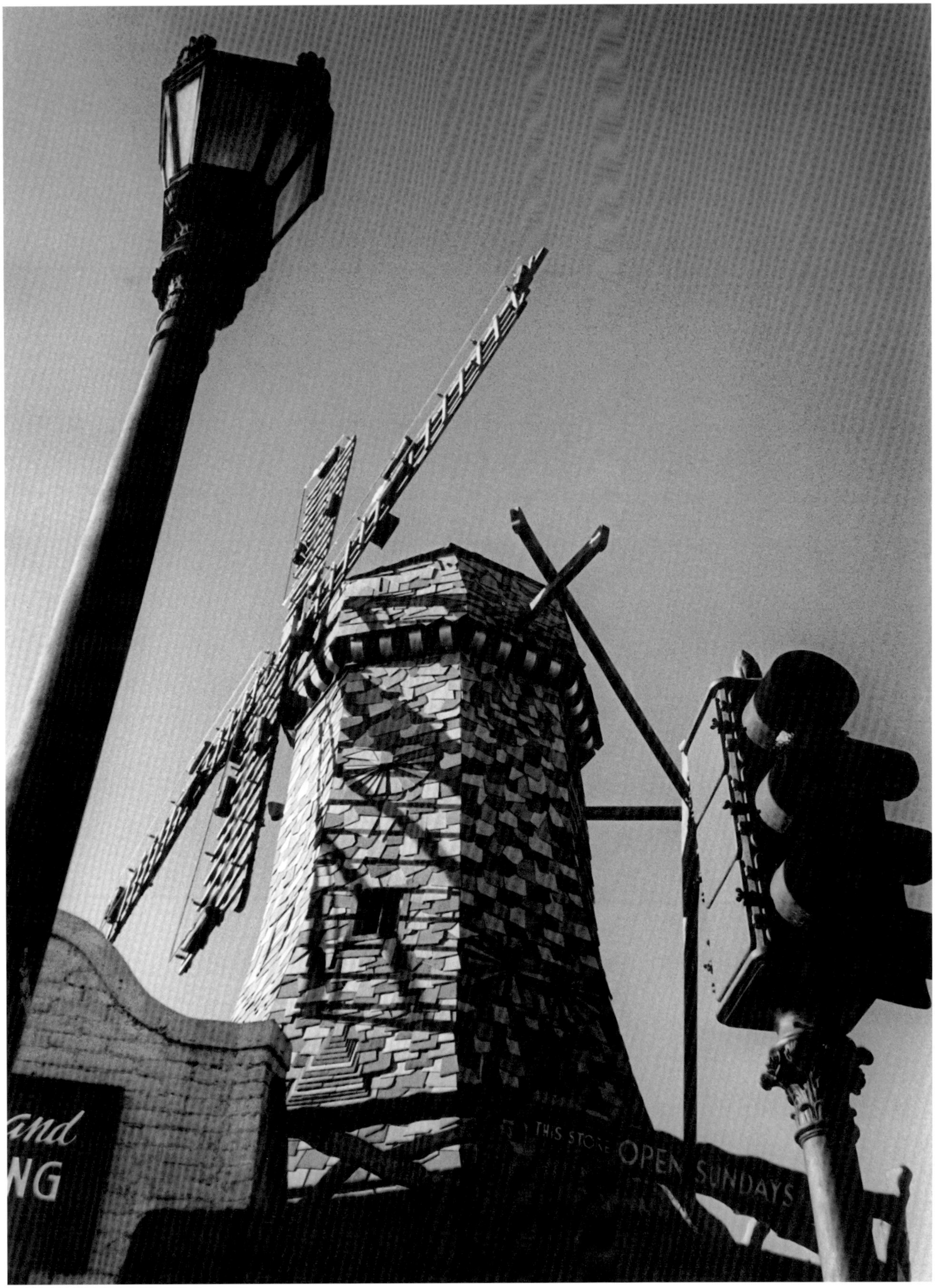
THIS STORE OPEN SUNDAYS

Street running toward Hollywood Hills, 1938

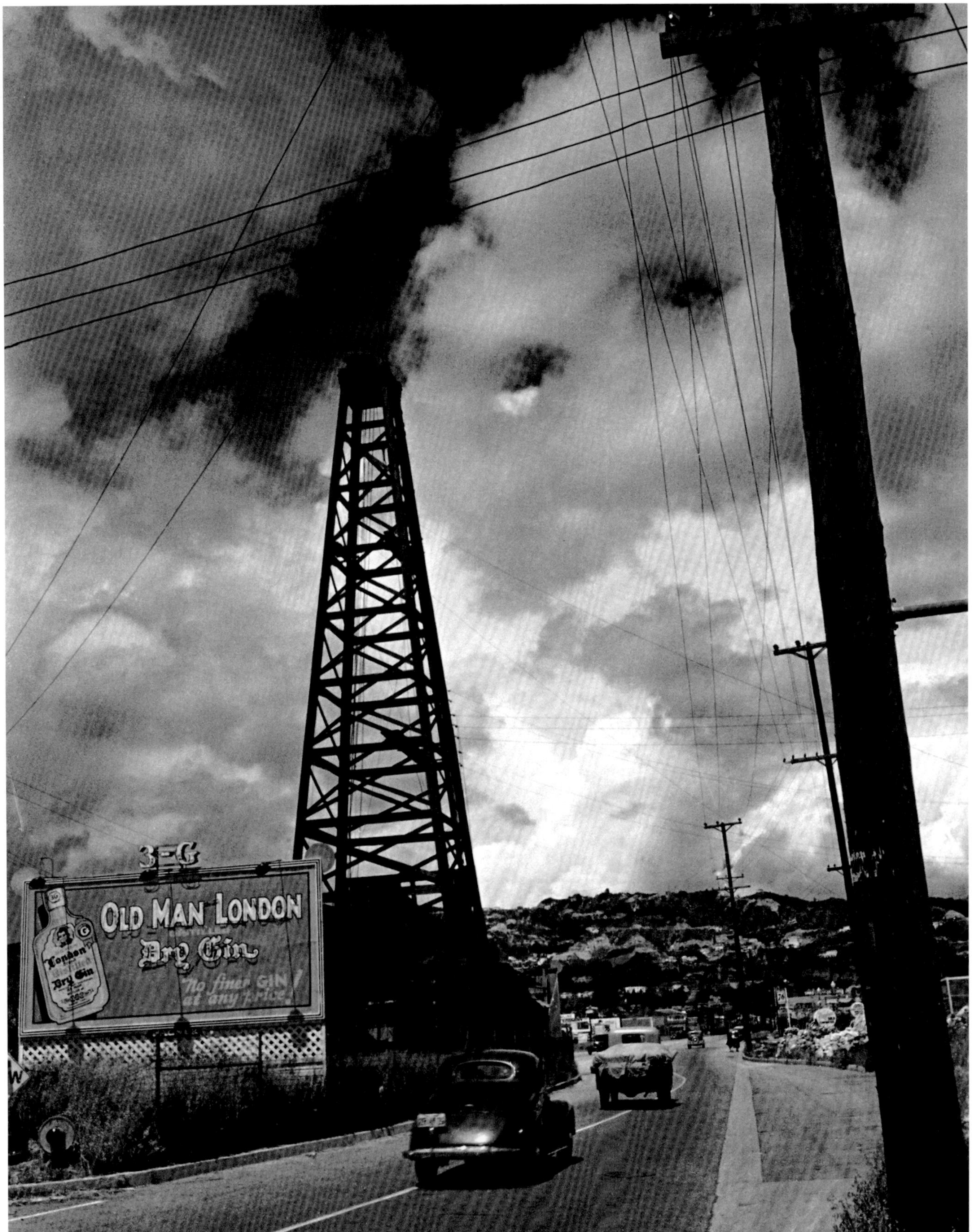
3-G
OLD MAN LONDON
Dry Gin
No finer GIN!
at any price!

Roger Edens, Hearst Ranch, San Simeon, 1938

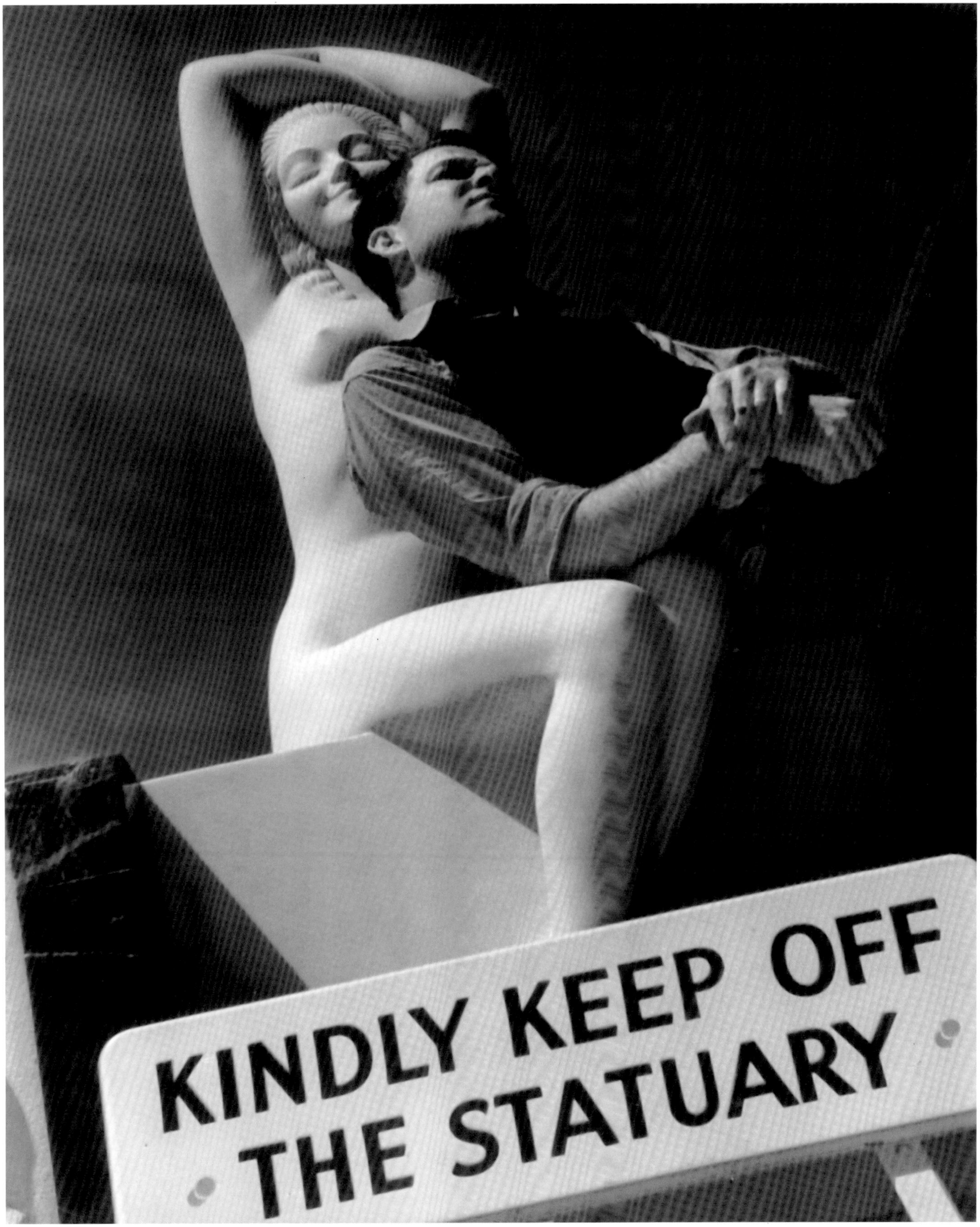
KINDLY KEEP OFF
THE STATUARY

Henry and Frances Fonda, 1936

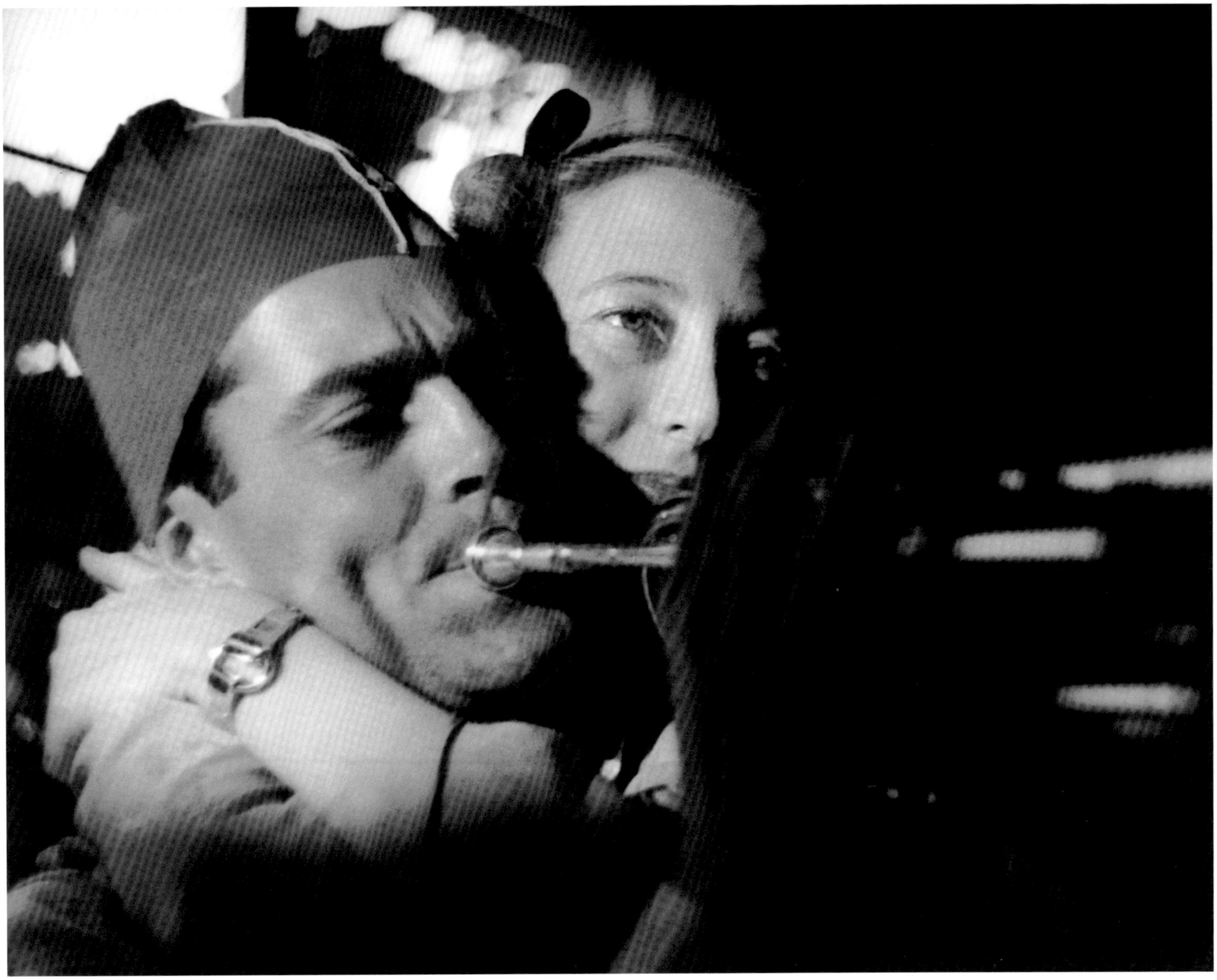

Kay and Jim Flood on the *Dorade,* 1938

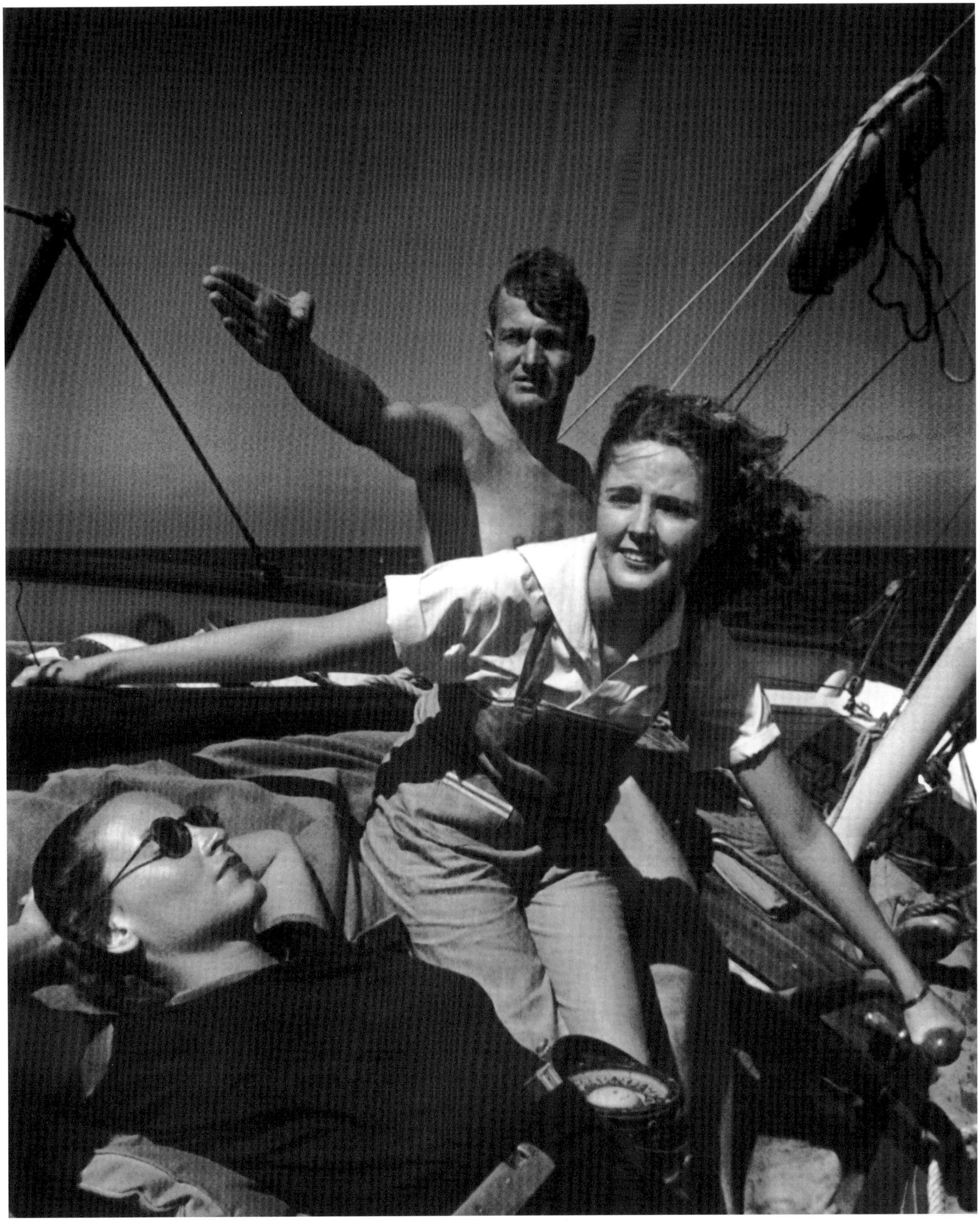

Libby Harben, 1938

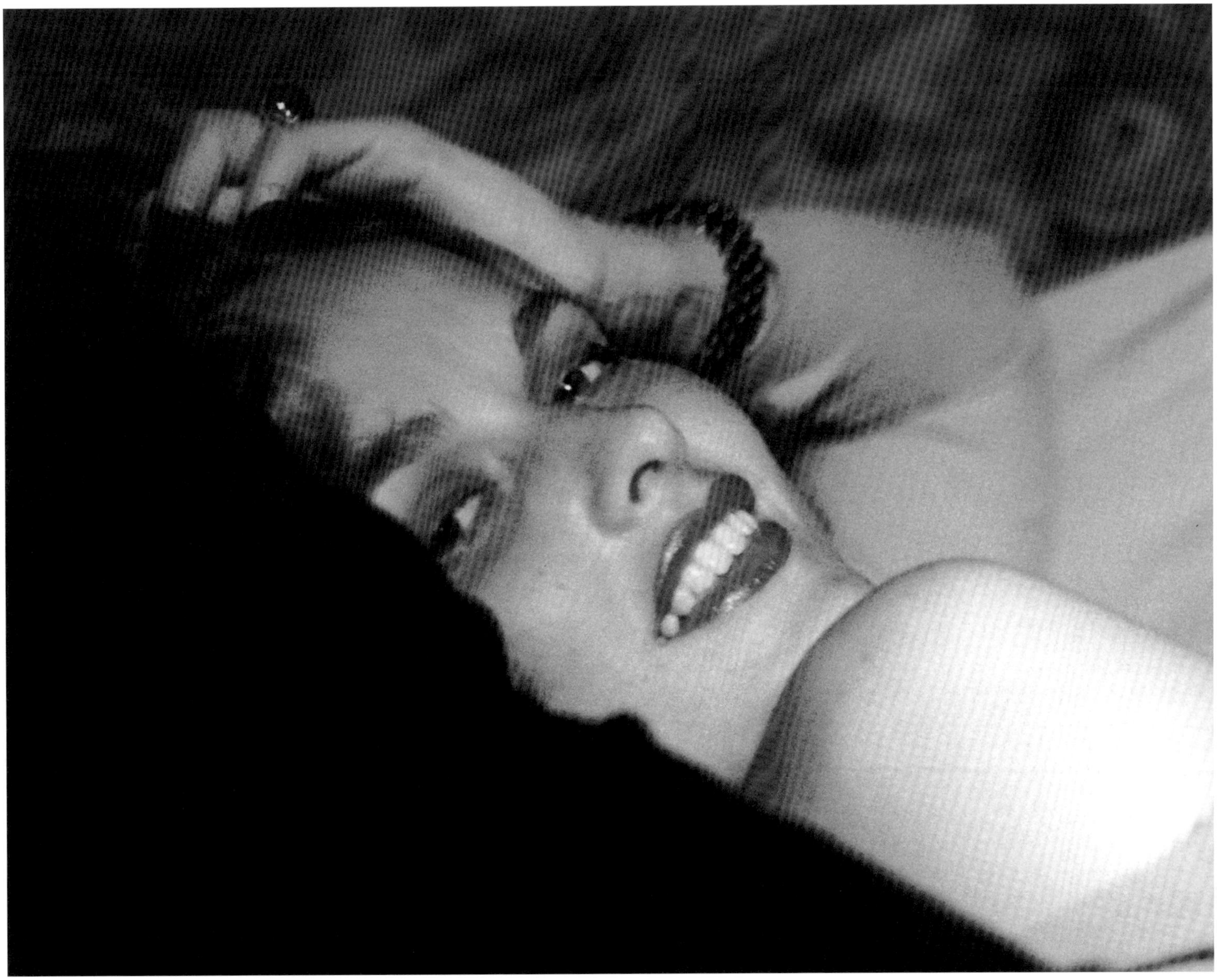

Albertina Rasch dancers at MGM, 1938

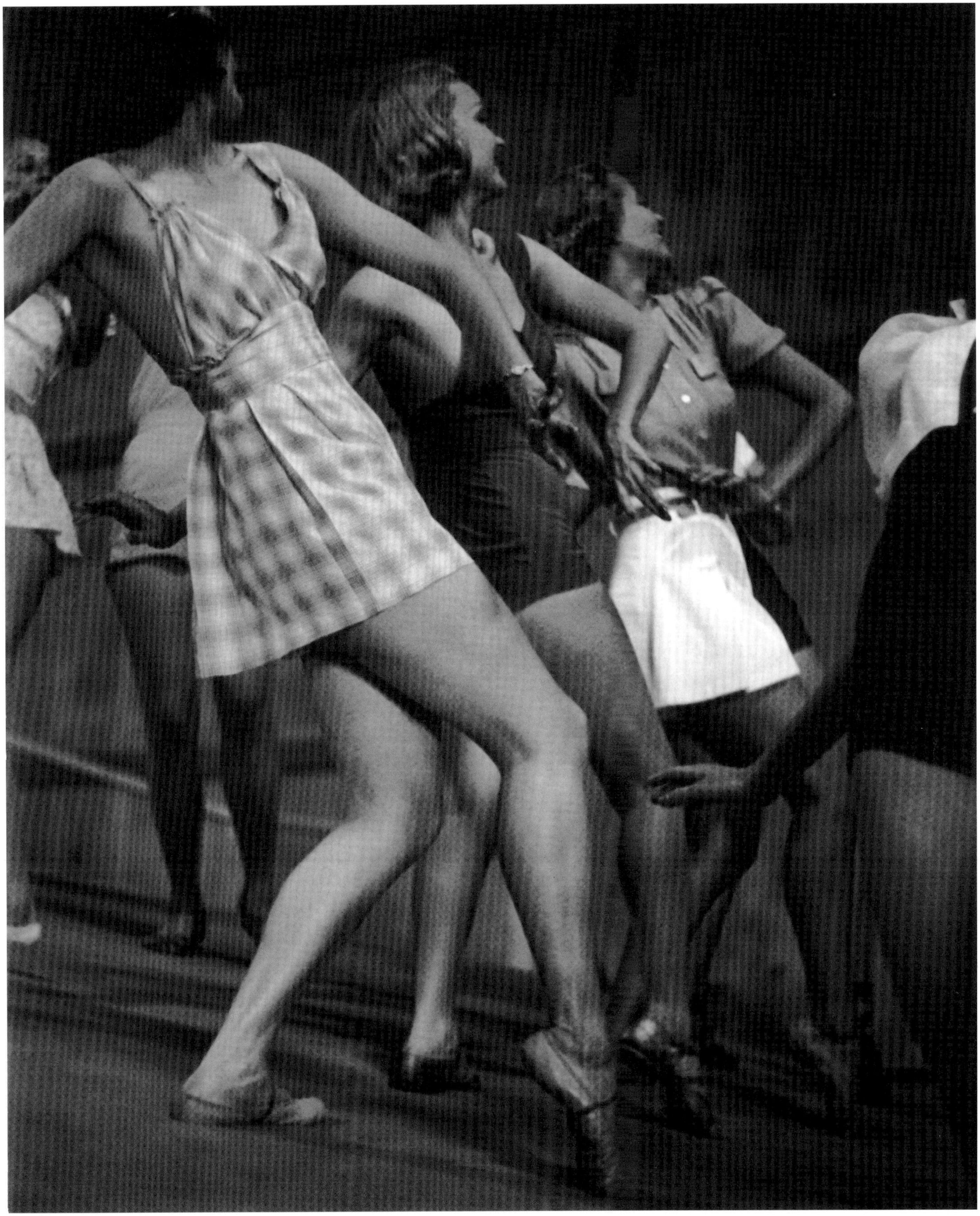

Extra on *Marie Antoinette* set reading *The Reporter,* 1938

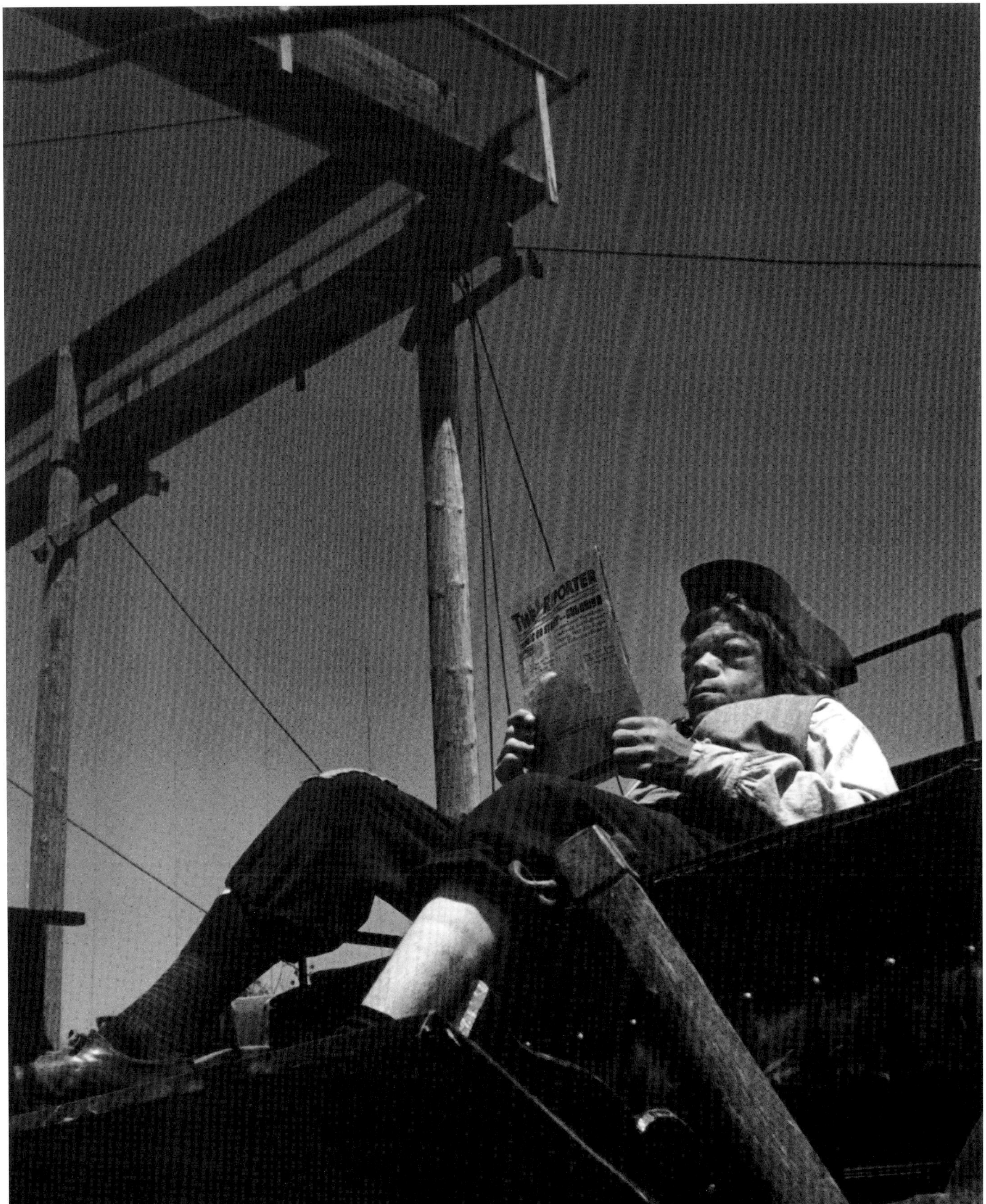

Henry Fonda, Jimmy Stewart, and John Swope in *The Spirit of '76*, 1937

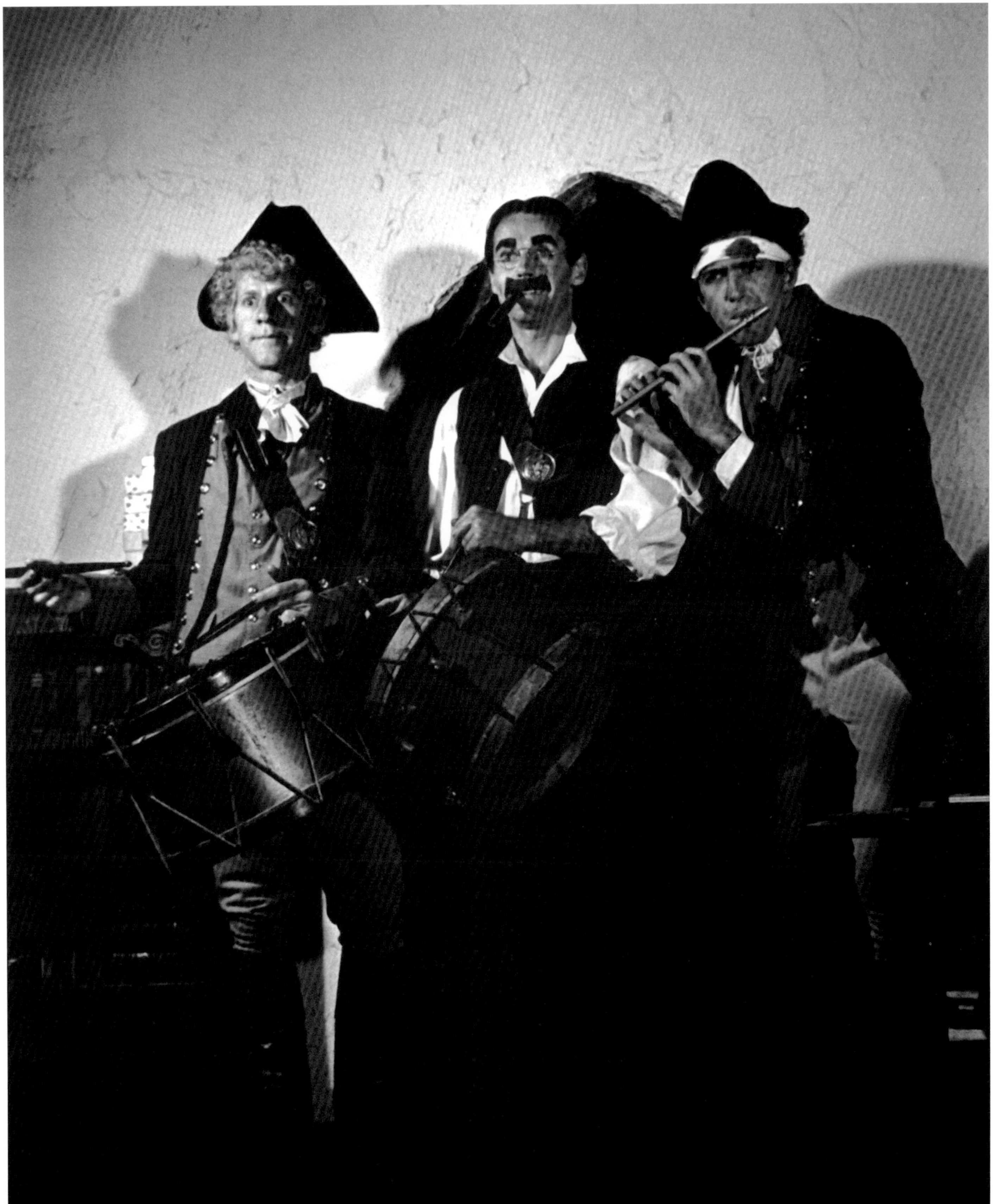

W. C. Fields and Mack Sennett on Oscar night, 1938

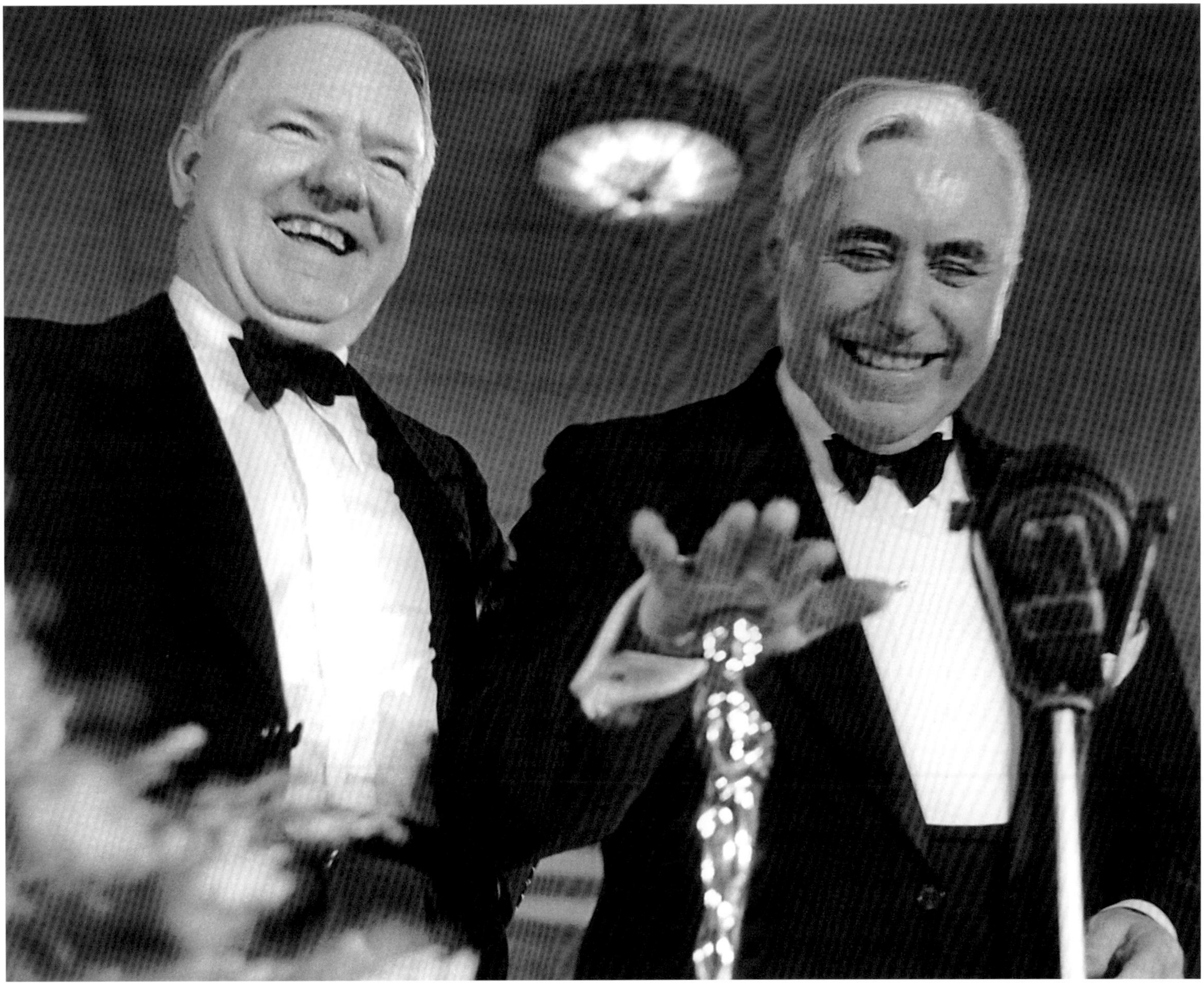

Louis B. Mayer, Luise Rainer, Mrs. Spencer Tracy, and Frank Capra, Oscar night, 1938

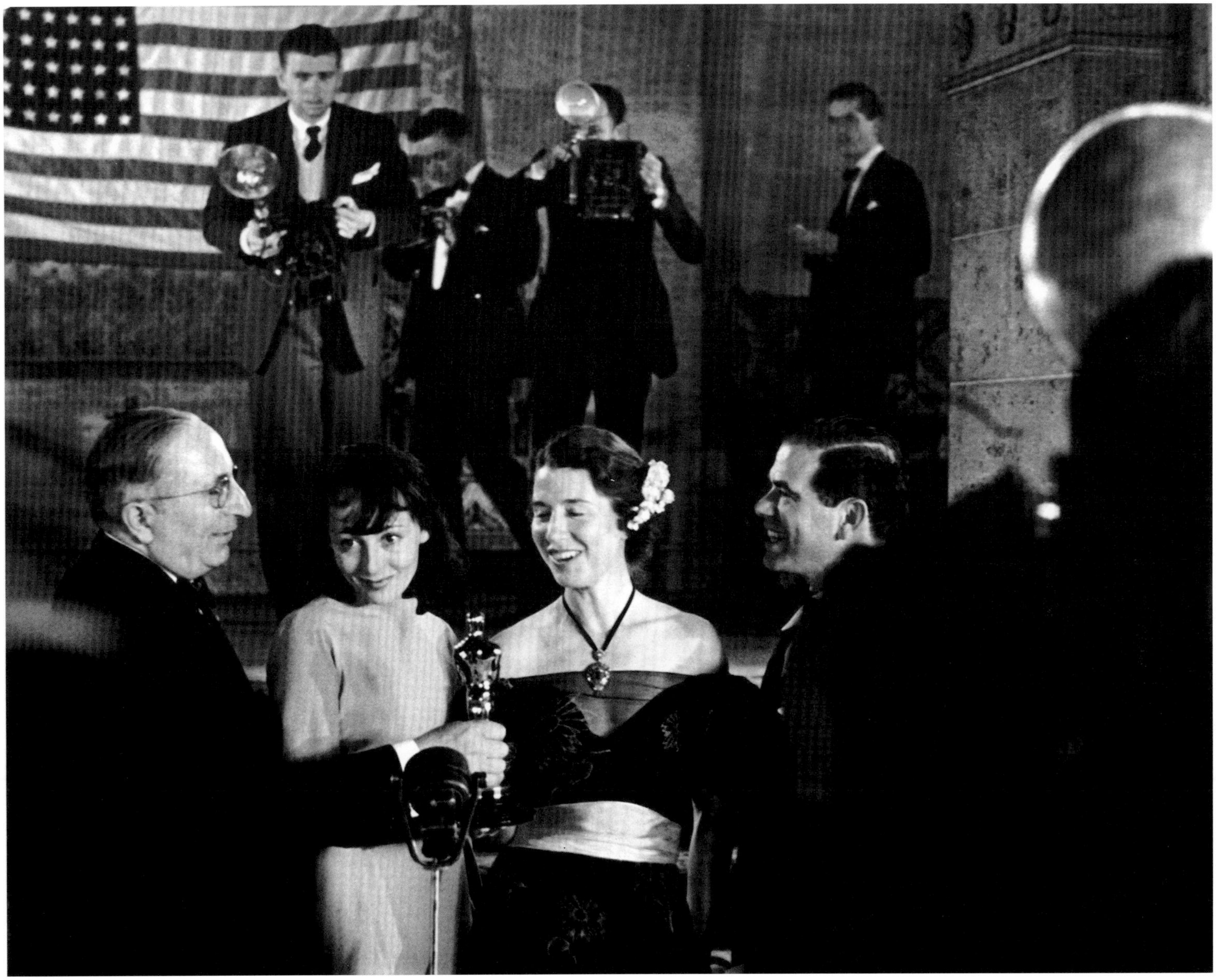

Extras in bed (two can live as cheaply as one), 1938

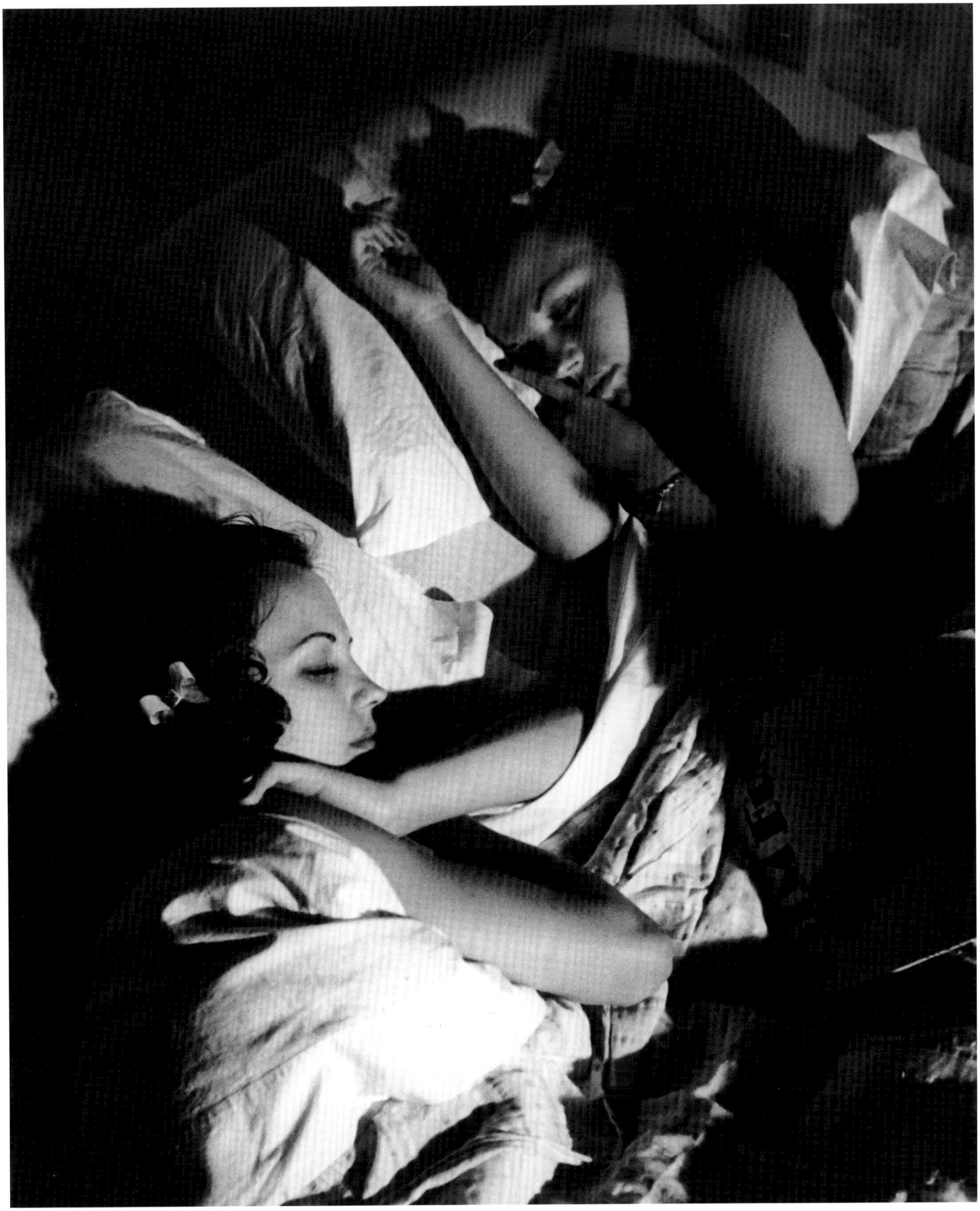

Extra washing clothes in sink, 1938

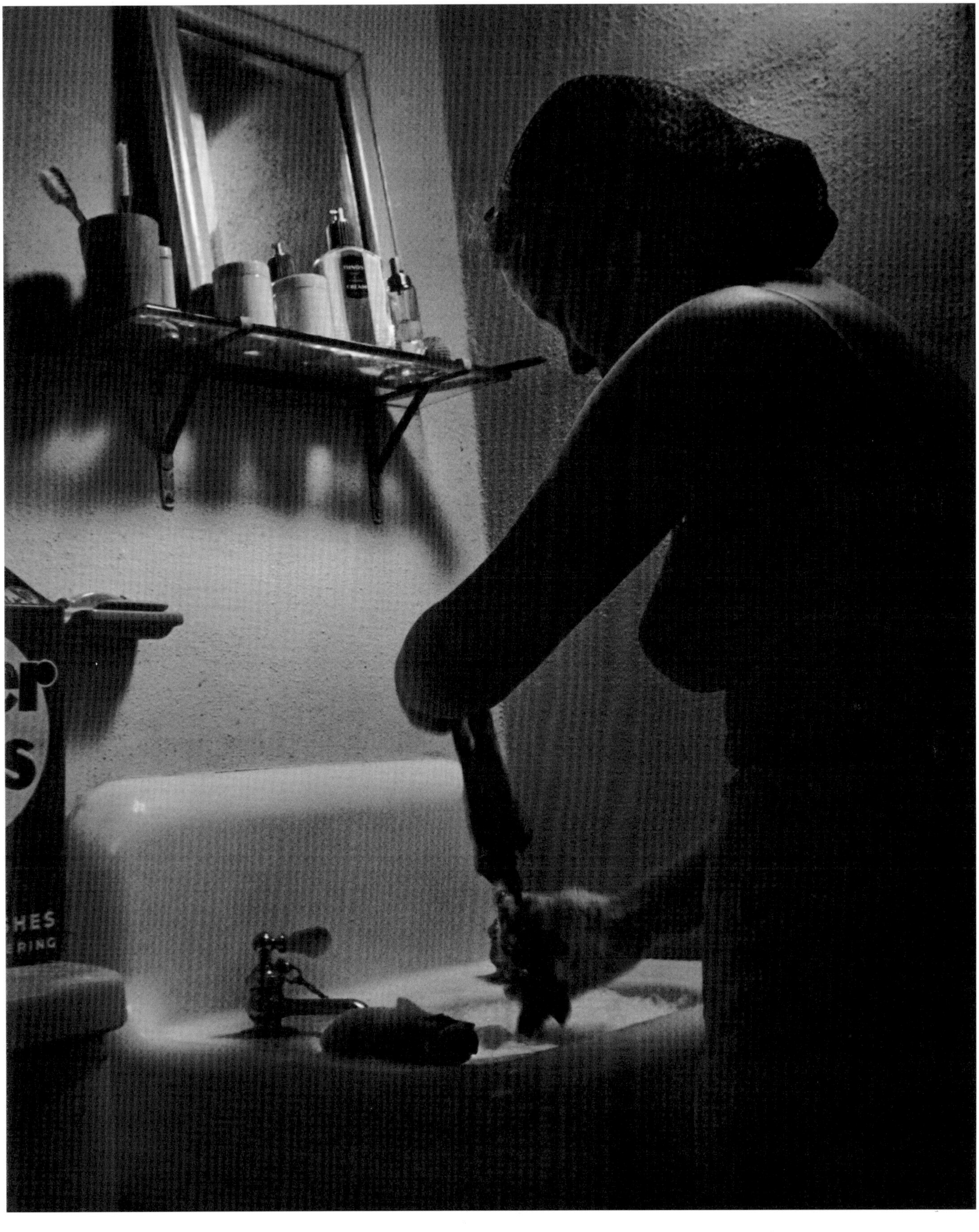

Opening night, 1938

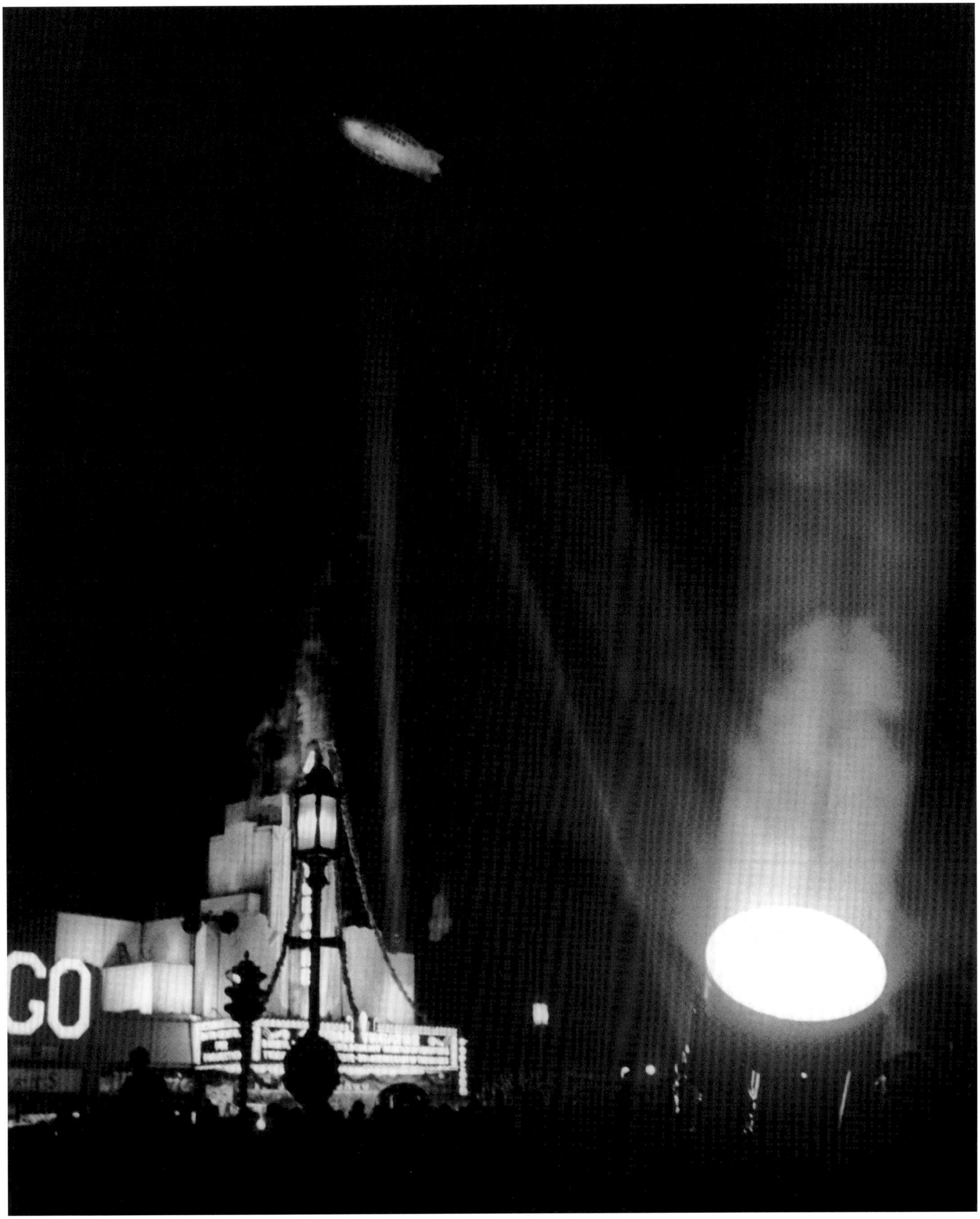
GO

Night view of Hollywood from hills, 1937

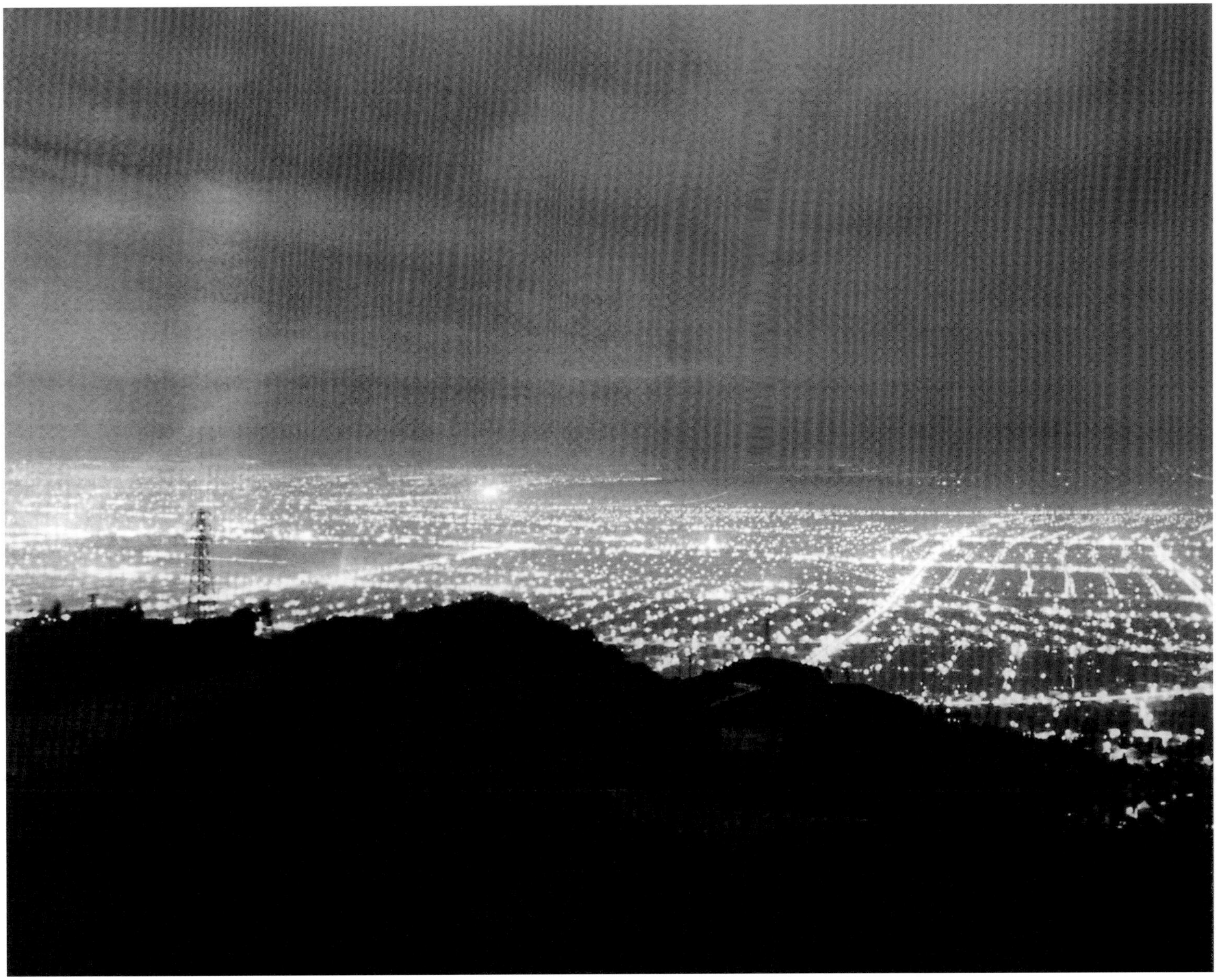

Urban backyard with a view of the City Hall Tower, Los Angeles, 1937

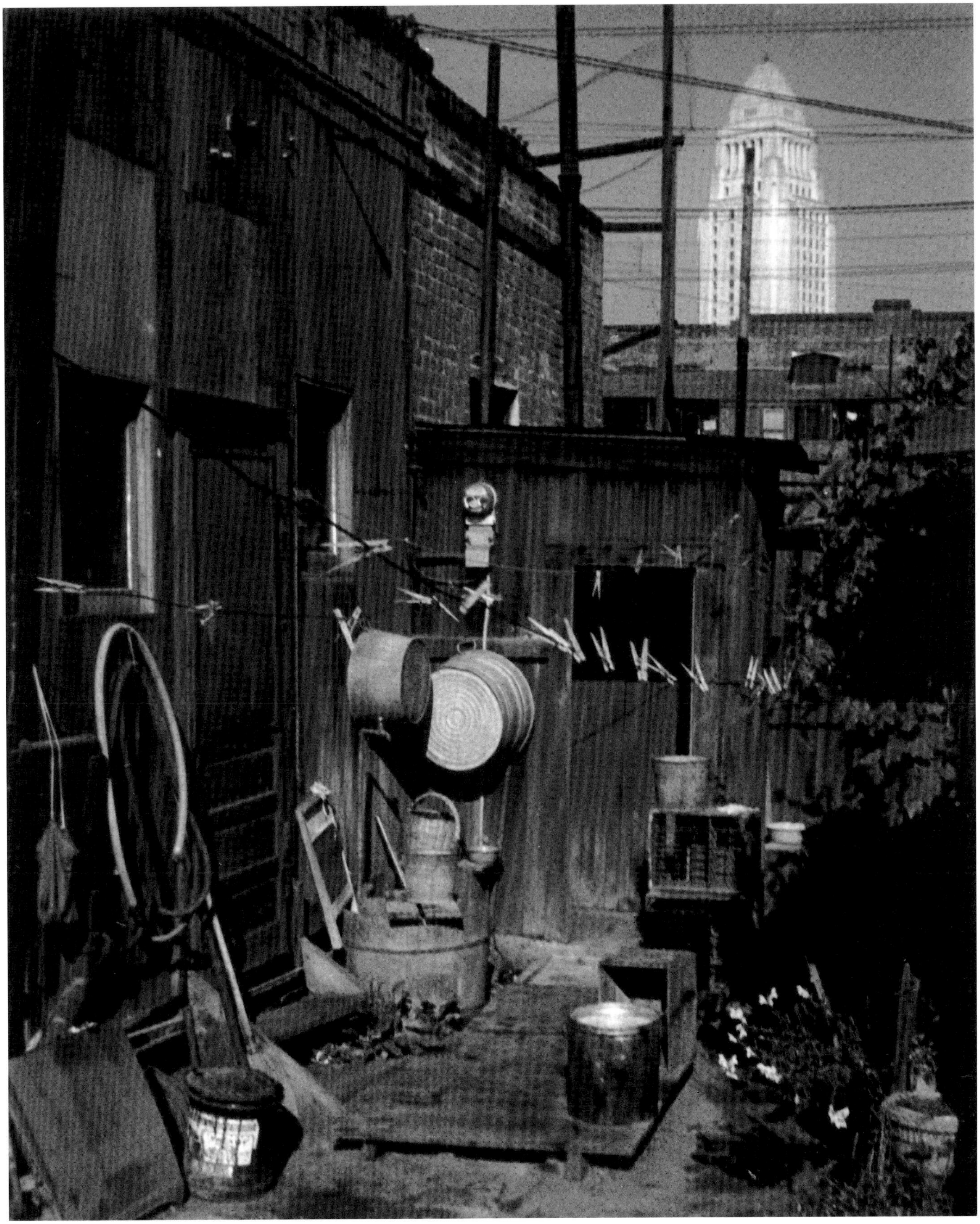